THE EIGHT LAWS OF SPIRITUAL RELEASE

Dr. D.L. Wallace, DDIV; PHD

Copyright © 2012 Dr. D.L. Wallace Ministries
All rights reserved.
Published by: *Majestic Kingdom Enterprise Group*

DEDICATION

This book is dedicated to my grandmother Rachel Wallace Randall, the greatest woman I have ever known. If it was not for her love and encouragement, I would not be the man I am today and nothing that I have done, or will ever do would be possible. Through her example, I have learned the value of education and that through faith and hard work anything is possible. My only regret is that she went home to be with the Lord before this work was finished.

TABLE OF CONTENTS

	Acknowledgments	*Pg 4*
1	*Introduction*	*Pg 5*
2	*The Law of Faithfulness*	*Pg 9*
3	*The Law of Sowing and Reaping*	*Pg 37*
4	*The Law of Transformation by Hearing*	*Pg 62*
5	*The Law of Forgiveness*	*Pg 88*
6	*The Law of Thanksgiving*	*Pg 116*
7	*The Law of Sacrifice*	*Pg 140*
8	*The Law of Seeking*	*Pg 168*
9	*The Law of Rest*	*Pg 195*

ACKNOWLEDGMENTS

As with any word of God there are many who have played a valuable role in bringing the vision for this book to life. To those at Greater Deliverance who bore with me as God developed this work I want to say thank you. To those who labored in prayer that the focus for this work would remain God's and that it would come to past and know that your effort did not go unnoticed.

1

INTRODUCTION

The timing of God is amazing!!!!!!! God sets every action and every activity done for our edification and His glory in their perfect place and releases them in His perfect time. Five years ago, as I was sitting at my desk preparing for a Sunday service I heard the spirit of God remind me of something that God had first revealed to me more than a decade earlier. He said "my people are dying because they do not know what I want from them" that statement still sends chills down my spine every time I hear it. This book is part of God solution to that problem.

Since the fall of Adam God in an overwhelming display of love has continually reached out to man calling us back to Him, back to a relationship based on His love and our willingness to follow. However as anyone who reads the Bible knows more often than not, we have failed to understand the measure of God's love or the response that He desires from us in return. As a result many of God expressions of love go unrecognized and many of His promises are left unfilled in the lives of those He loves and I presume love Him.

This work was written through His inspiration in an effort to reveal and examine eight laws of spiritual release. These laws which serve as gateways, allow us to enter into the blessings of God or at least enter into them on a deeper level. In writing this book, I am not suggesting that these eight laws are the only such laws or that they are the most important, but rather offer them as a starting point of a journey of discovery of the laws or principles upon which life in the Kingdom of God is based.

In writing this book I do not presume to suggest that my treatment or examination of these laws is exhaustive because it would take more than a hundred lifetimes to discuss all that God has said on any single law. This book is not a call for legalism, but a call to relationship based on the truth of God's word and God's nature.

It is my hope that those who read this book will be provoked to examine what they understand about both the Bible and their personal experiences and begin to search for areas where they may be able to apply these laws in their lives in order to receive more of the blessings that God intends for them and perhaps gain a better understanding as to why some of the events in their lives may have transpired the way they have or have re-occurred as often as they have.

Most of all it is my prayer that those who read the material that follows will develop a more intense love for and commitment to God and find the strength and courage to live for God based on His laws in a way that they may not have before.

THE EIGHT LAWS OF SPIRITUAL RELEASE

2

THE LAW OF FAITHFULNESS

The Law of Faithfulness

The law of Faithfulness provides that the blessings we receive tomorrow will be determined by how we handle the opportunities and instructions we are presented today.

D.L. Wallace

Throughout the body of Christ there is an awakening to a fuller truth of not only the measure of God's love towards us, but also the fullness of God's plan for us. In Jeremiah 29:11 The Prophet Jeremiah writes to the nation of Israel suffering Babylonia captivity "I know the thoughts that I think towards you, saith the Lord, thoughts of peace, and not of evil, to give you an expected end." (KJV) or as expressed in the (AMP) "For I know the thoughts and plans I have for you, says the Lord, thoughts and plans for welfare and peace, and not for evil, to give you hope in your final out come." Further in Psalms 35:27, the writer declares" let them shout for joy, and be glad, that favor my righteous cause: yea, let them say continually, let the Lord be magnified, which hath pleasure in the prosperity of His People" or as it is expressed in the Amplified translation, " Let those who favor my righteous cause and have pleasure in my righteousness shout for joy and be glad, and say continually, Let the Lord be magnified, who takes pleasure in the prosperity of His servants" In addition teachings like the Prayer of Jabez by Dr. Bruce Wilkinson which is based upon the prayer which is found in 1 Chronicles 4:10 and provides "and Jabez called on the God of Israel, saying, oh that thou would bless me indeed, and enlarge my coast, and that thine hand might be with me, and that thou wouldest keep me from evil, that it may not grieve me! And God granted him that which he requested." Or as the Amplified translations states " Jabez cried to the God of Israel, saying, Oh that you would bless me and enlarge my border, and that your hand might be with me, and you would keep me from evil so it might not hurt me! And God granted his request" provide clear Biblical support to the growing expectation in the Body of Christ that God desires to fulfill the promises contained in Deuteronomy 28: 3-14, which provides as follows "You will be Blessed in the city and blessed in the country. The fruit of your womb will be blessed, and the crops of your land and the young of your livestock the calves of your herds and the lambs of your flocks. Your basket and your kneading trough will be blessed. You will be blessed when you come in and blessed when you go out. The Lord will grant that the enemies who rise up against you will be defeated before you. They will come at you from one direction but flee from you in seven. The Lord your God will bless you in the land He has given you. The Lord will establish you as His holy people, as he promised you on oath, if you keep the commands of the Lord your God and walk in his ways. Then all the people on earth will see that you are called by the name of the Lord, and they will fear you. The Lord will grant you abundant prosperity – in the fruit of your womb, the young of your livestock and the crops of your ground-in the land he swore to your fathers to give you. The Lord will open the heavens, the storehouse of his bounty, to send rain on your land in season and to bless all the work of your hands you will lend to many nations but will not borrow from none. The Lord will make you the head, not the tail. If you pay attention to the commands of the Lord your God that I give you this day and carefully follow them, you will always be at the top, never at the bottom. Do not turn aside from any of the commands I give you today, to the right or to the left, following other Gods and serving them" or as the Amplified translation states " Blessed shall you be in the city, and blessed shall you be in the field. Blessed shall be the fruit of your body, and the fruit of your ground, and the fruit of your beasts, the increase of your cattle, and the young of your flock. Blessed shall be your basket and your kneading trough. Blessed shall you be when you come in, and blessed shall you be when you go out. The Lord shall cause your enemies who rise up against you to be defeated before your face; they shall come out against you one way, and flee before you seven ways. The Lord shall command the blessing upon you in your store house, and in all that you undertake; and He will bless you in the land which the Lord your God gives you. The Lord will establish you as a people holy to Himself, as He has sworn to you, if you keep the commandments of the Lord your God, and walk in His ways. And all the people of the earth shall see that you are called by the name [and in the presence of] the Lord; and they shall be afraid of you. And the Lord shall make you have a surplus of prosperity, through the fruit of your body, of your livestock, and of your ground, in the land which the Lord swore to your fathers to give you. The Lord shall open to you His good treasury, the heavens to give the rain of your land in its season, and to bless all the work of your hand; and you shall lend to many nations, but you shall not borrow. And the Lord shall make you the head, and not the tail; and shall make you above only, and not beneath. If you heed the commandments of the Lord your God which I command you this day, and are watchful to do them And you shall not go aside from any of the words which I command you this day, to the right hand or to the left, to go after other gods to serve them." which promise blessings and elevations. However, as clear as Gods intentions towards us are, it is equally clear that the manifestations, the blessings and elevations promised by God require more than mere desire on our part. They require faithfulness. But what is faithfulness? The word faithfulness or the derivative of its root word faith appears in scripture approximately 528 times of which 84 are found in the old testament and 444 are found in the new testament. In examining each of the four Hebrew words used in scripture which translates into the English words faith, faithful or faithfulness it becomes clear that the term faithfulness connotes trustworthiness, steadfastness and consistency. Similarly the two Greek words which translate into the English words faith, faithful or faithfulness connotes trustworthiness or consistency. Therefore, to be faithful or to be deemed to possess faithfulness is to operate in a consistently trustworthy manner. In Matt 25: 14-29 Jesus while teaching on the kingdom begins teaching on the value of faithfulness by establishing the basis of God's expectation. In verse 14, He describes the subjects of the lesson as God's servants. In this simple but very direct statement Jesus makes it clear that the standard upon which we are judged is not established by us or by others around us, but rather by God and God alone. Therefore, it is only God who can determine whether we are faithful. This fact is supported through scripture and is at least implicitly address by the Apostle Paul in the 8 chapter of the book of Romans verses 29-31, 33 where he writes "For whom (God) foreknow, he also did predestinate to be conformed to the image of his son, that he might be the first born among many brethren. Moreover whom he did predestinate, them he also called: and whom he called, them he also justified: and whom he justified, them he also glorified.

What shall we then say to these things? If God be for us, who can be against us? Who shall lay anything to the charge of God's elect? It is God that justifies" or as it is stated in the Amplified translation " For those whom He foreknew- of whom He was aware and loved beforehand- He also destined from the beginning (foreordaining them) to be molded into the image of His Son [and share inwardly His likeness], that He might become the first-born among many brethren. And those whom He thus foreordained He also called; and those whom He called He also justified- acquitted, made righteous, putting them in right standing with Himself. And those whom He justified He also glorified – raising them to a heavenly dignity and condition [state of being]. What then shall we say to [all] of this? If God be for us, who [can be] against us?- who can be our foe, if God is on our side?" "Who can bring any charge against God's elect [when it is] God who justifies- who puts us in right relation to Himself? (who shall forward and accuse or impeach those whom God has chosen? Will God who acquits us?)". In verse 30 and 33 the Apostle Paul makes it clear that God and God alone has reserved the right to judge the faithfulness of those He has chosen. The question of who judges the faithfulness of God's servants becomes of particular importance in a society and a culture where truth and right and wrong have become relative and societal norms promote standards of conduct that are often contrary to the express will of God and were socially acceptable conduct may be unbiblical. Especially in situations where some if not many of those that stand in positions of spiritual leadership have adopted worldly definitions of success, sources of identity and in some cases have ignored if not completely abandoned the teaching of the bible especially in areas of Christian services, charity, humility and personal disciplines. In point of fact the History of Christianity paints a clear picture of the danger of living and perhaps more importantly serving in order to satisfy the expectation of anyone other than God while at the same time highlighting the virtue and necessity of living a life faithful to God even when doing so will result in our being misunderstood and rejected by men. This point becomes clear as the Apostle Paul warned against seeking acceptance from any source other than God in the first two verses of the 12th Chapter of the book of Romans when he wrote "I beseech you therefore, brethren, by the mercies of God, that ye present your bodies a living sacrifice, holy acceptable unto God, which is your reasonable service and be not conformed to this world: but be ye transformed by the renewing of your mind, that ye may prove what is that good, and acceptable, and perfect, will of God" or as the Amplified states " I APPEAL to you therefore, brethren, and beg of you

The Eight Laws of Spiritual Release

in view of [all] the mercies of God, to make a decisive dedication of your bodies- presenting all your members and faculties- as a living sacrifice, holy (devoted, consecrated) and well pleasing to God, which is your reasonable (rational, intelligent) service and spiritual worship. Do not be conformed to this world- this age, fashioned after and adapted to its external, superficial customs. But be transformed (changed) by the [entire] renewal of your mind- by its new ideals and its new attitude — so that you may prove [for yourselves] what is the good and acceptable and perfect will of God, even the thing which is good and acceptable and perfect [in His sight for you]."

In short the determination of whether a person is faithful is God's and God's alone. This should be a source of great comfort to anyone who seeks to be deemed faithful in the sight of God. To some the thought of being deemed faithful by God, the Father and creator of all things, the almighty, all knowing and all powerful God might be a little overwhelming and it might seem as if being deemed faithful in the sight of man would be more obtainable. However, that is simply not true, it is not true because while man's standards are both generic and arbitrary, Gods are not and while man's standards are harsh, impersonal and imposed without regard to those seeking to live and be defined by them, God's are based in mercy, desiring to produce the best in us and for us and take into consideration our human frailty and our infirmities.

One of the clearest examples of this point is found in the 16th Chapter of the first book of Samuel. The 16th Chapter of the first book of Samuel recounts the story of God's choice of David as King of Israel. God's Prophet Samuel was instructed by God to go to the house of Jesse because God had chosen one of Jesse's sons to be king of Israel however God did not reveal which son He had chosen to Samuel. When Samuel arrives at the home of Jessie, Samuel prepared a sacrifice and sanctifies Jessie and his sons and calls them to the sacrifice. In 1 Sam 16: 6-7 the Bible declares " and it came to pass, when they were come, that he (Samuel) looked on Eliab, and said Surely the Lord anointed is before him. But the Lord said unto Samuel, Look not on his countenance, or on the height of his stature; because I have refused him: for the Lord seeth not as man seeth; for man looketh on the outward appearance, but the Lord looketh on the heart" or as the Amplified translations states " When they had come, he looked on Eliab [the eldest son], and said surely the Lord's anointed is before Him. But the Lord said to Samuel, Look not on his appearance or at the height of his stature, for I have rejected him; for the Lord sees not as man sees; for man looks on the outward appearance, but the Lord looks on the heart." In this scripture we see the danger of living and being judge by a standard of man and not of God. Here, as is usually the case, man's standards are generic and arbitrary and judge us based on impersonal criteria which fail to reflect our unique value to God or the Kingdom of God. The world's expectation and standards and are imposed without regard to our God given gifts, our desires, experiences or the content of our heart, or as God declared man looks on the outward appearance, but the Lord judges the heart and it is in the Heart where faithfulness is ultimately determined. It is interesting to note that Samuel's assumption was quite reasonable under the circumstance. Eliab was the eldest Son of Jessie in a culture where the eldest son was entitled to the best of his fathers possessions and often received a double portion upon inheritance. In addition, as the eldest child, Eliab was most likely placed in a leadership position within the family and would be seem as the most capable of all Jessie's sons. In addition, he looked the part, he was tall and of considerable size, most certainly larger and more commanding in appearance than Jessie's youngest son David. However, God was not simply looking for a king for appearance sake but was looking for a king with a servant's heart one whose faith in God would overrule his fear, a king who possessed courage, a king who would be a protector of God's chosen, a king who would deliver them from persecution. But inside Eliab's impressive appearance was the heart of a coward, the heart of a man who would seek to protect himself above God's people or God's honor. He was a man whose heart was focused on himself and not on God. David may not have looked the part, he may not have had a stature that impressed those around him but he had a heart that impressed God. What Samuel did not realize was that in the eyes of God faithfulness and ones qualifications are all a matter of the heart. Look at the emphasis God places on the heart of His people in Jeremiah 29:14. In Jeremiah 29:12-14 God through the Prophet Jeremiah declares the preconditions of the nation of Israel's deliverance from Babylonian captivity and the restoration of their Kingdom as follows. "Then shall ye call upon me, and ye shall go and pray unto me, and I will hearken unto you and ye shall seek me, and find me, when ye shall search for me with all your heart, and I will be found of you, saith the Lord: and I will turn away your captivity , and I will gather you from all the nation's, and from all the places whither I have driven you, saith the Lord; and I will bring you again into the place whence I caused you to be carried away captive." Or as the Amplified states "Then you will call upon me, and you will come and pray to Me, and I will hear and heed you. Then you will seek Me, inquire for and require Me [as a vital necessity] and find Me, when you search for Me with all your heart. I will be found by you, says the Lord, and I will release you from captivity and gather you from all the nations and all the places to which I have driven you, say the Lord, and I will bring you again to the place from which I caused you to be carried away captive." It is interesting to note that not only does God place His emphasis upon the condition of their heart as oppose to the outward expression of religious practices but also makes their faithfulness to the first commandment "thou shall have no Gods before me" a prerequisite or a condition to God restoring them to the position of ruler ship as a nation. This is particularly important because the primary cause of the Babylonian captivity was the nation of Israel's idolatry. This emphasis by God on the condition of the heart of man is further emphasis in Matt 22: 34-40. In the 34-40 verses of the 22nd Chapter of the Gospel according to Matthew Jesus is questioned by an unnamed Pharisee who seeking to force Jesus to choose one of the commandment over the other asked Jesus which of the commandment was most important to observe, in other words what is the best outward expression of faithfulness to Judge man by, and in response Jesus, said "Thou shalt love the Lord thy God with all thy heart, and with all thy soul, and with all thy mind. This is the first and great commandment and the second is like unto it, Thou shalt love thy neighbor as thy self. On these two commandments hang all the law and the prophets or as it is stated in the Amplified translation "Now when the Pharisees heard that He had silenced (muzzled) the Sadducees, they gathered together; and one of their number, a lawyer, asked Him a question to test Him. Teacher, which kind of commandment is great and important—the principal kind—in the Law? [some are light; which are heavy?]. And He replied to him. You shall love the Lord your God with all your heart, and with all your soul, and with all you mind (intellect). This is the great (most important, principal) and first commandment. And the second is like it, you shall love your neighbor as [you do] yourself. These two commandments sum up and upon them depends all the Law and the prophets." In other words it is the content of one's heart and not simply the activity of ones hands that determine faithfulness to God, which is the essence of the Apostle Paul's statement in the 1st verse of the 11th Chapter of the Book of Hebrews. In the 25th Chapter of the Gospel according to Matthew Jesus set forth the basis for His standard of faithfulness. In the 25th Chapter of the Gospel according to Matthew Jesus teaches the law of faithfulness through the use of the Parable about the talents. In that

Parable Jesus tell the story of three servants each of whom have been given talents by their master, In this parable the talents are used as a form of monetary currency, however it is commonly understood that the talents given to the servants by their master serve as a metaphor for the giftedness with which God has given all mankind in general. Further in the parable we are taught that each of the three servants are given a differing series or measure of gifts, the first having been given five talents, the second having been given two talents and the third and final servant having been given one. It is also important to note that each of the three servants were given their respective talents in the same area, at the same time and under the same circumstance which serve to signify that each of the three servants were given the same opportunity to succeed. If we examine this point in the context of greater biblical truth it becomes evident that the weight of scripture gives credence to this truth. First the bible teaches us we were all born in sin and shaped in iniquity and as a result each of us has a sin nature which opposes God will and desires sin. Second each of us has the opportunity to hear the Gospel of Jesus Christ and by believing in our heart the Lord Jesus and confessing that God raised Him from the dead, receive salvation through faith in Jesus Christ, Third each of us have been given gifts, (Rom 12:6-7) and (1

Corinthians 12:4-11) and the opportunity through the Holy Spirit to develop the same fruit (Gal 5:22-23) for God's glory and man's edification, and the same assignment (Matt 28:19-20) all of which make each of us equally capable of proving ourselves faithful to God. Some might question the assertion that we are given an equal opportunity to proving ourselves faithful and in doing so point to those whose lives began under disadvantages if not tragic circumstances. In point of fact many in the world today and even some within the body of Christ point to the harsh realities of single parent households, poverty, violent and crime filled communities, physical, emotional and sexual abuse as justifications for many not only failing to live a life which demonstrates faithfulness to God, but also of the adoption of a different standard for those in our society deems to be either irreparable damaged or who find themselves in circumstances so disadvantageous that the standard set for them by God should be redefined for them. I disagree, I disagree, I disagree and I believe that those who make this argument are not basing it on any perceived inability of those they presume to protect from the imposition of unrealistic expectations, but rather a lack on any true Biblical faith in God. In the 11th thru 13th verse of the 4th Chapter of the book of Philippians, the Apostle Paul describing the frequent lack that he experiences while fulfilling the assignment given to Him by Jesus Christ remarked in the 13th verse "I can do all things through Christ which strengthens me." Or as it is stated in the Amplified translation "I have strength for all things in Christ who empowers me—I am ready for anything and equal to anything through Him who infuses inner strength into me, [that is I am self-sufficient in Christ's sufficiency]. This statement echoes what Jesus Himself taught us in Matt 19:26 when He said "With man this is impossible, but with God all things are possible." Is the basis of all Biblical faith without which there can be no true belief in healing, deliverance or even salvation. In addition scripture is full of examples of people who were born into poverty, insignificance, bondage and with God's help and guidance faithfully serve God and fulfill God's assigned work for them. One such person is Moses. The Bible teaches us that Moses was born during an extremely difficult time in the history of the nation of Israel. A time when the Egyptians so feared and despised them that Pharaoh devised a plan to weaken if not utterly destroy them. In the first Chapter of the book of Exodus verses 8-16, 22 the Bible declares "Now there arose up a new King over Egypt, which knew not Joseph, and he said unto his people, Behold, the people of the children of Israel are more and mightier than we: come on, let us deal wisely with them; lest they multiply, and it come to pass, that, when there falleth out any war, they join also unto our enemies, and fight against us, and so get them up out of the land. Therefore they did set over them taskmaster to afflict them with their burdens, and they built for Pharaoh treasure cities, Pithom, and Raamses. But the more they afflicted them, the more they multiplied and grew. And they were grieved because of the children of Israel. And the Egyptians made the children of Israel to serve with rigor: And they made their lives bitter with hard bondage, in mortar, and in brick, and in all manner of service in the field: all their service, wherein they made them serve, was with rigor. And the King of Egypt spake to the Hebrew midwives, of which the name of the one was Shiphrah, and the of the other Puah: And he said, when ye do the office of a midwife to the Hebrew women, and see them upon the stool; if it be a son, then ye shall kill him: but if it be a daughter, then she shall live. And Pharaoh charged all his people, saying, every son that is born ye shall cast into the river." Or as it is stated in the Amplified translation " Now a new King arose over Egypt, who did not know Joseph. He said to his people, Behold, the Israelites are too many and too mighty for us — they outnumber us both in people and in strength. Come, let us deal shrewdly with them, lest they multiply more, and, should war befall us, they join our enemies, fight against us, and escape out of the land. So they set over [the Israelites] taskmasters to afflict and oppress them with [increased] burdens. And [the Israelites] built Pithom and Raames as store cities for Pharaoh. But the more [the Egyptians] oppressed them, the more they multiplied and expanded, so that [the Egyptians] were vexed and alarmed because of the Israelites. And the Egyptians reduced the Israelites to severe slavery. They made their work bitter with hard service, in mortar, brick, and all kinds of work in the field. All their service was with harshness and severity. Then the King of Egypt said to the Hebrew Midwives, of whom one was named Shiprah and the other Puah. When you act as midwife to the Hebrew women, and see them on the birthstool, if it is a son, you shall kill him; but if it is a daughter, she shall live." "Then Pharaoh charged all his people, saying Every son born [to the Hebrews] you shall cast into the river [Nile], but every daughter you shall allow to live. "The Bible further provides that "and when she (Moses mother) and bare a son: and when she saw him that he was a godly child, she hid him three months. And when she could no longer hide him she took for him an ark of bulrushes, and daubed it with slime and with pitch, and put the child therein; and she laid it in the flags by the river's brink. (Exodus 2:2-3) In addition the bible teaches us that Moses was consumed with anger which resulted in his commission of murder in order to protect a fellow member of the nation of Israel. In Exodus 2:11-14 the Bible declares "and it came to pass in those days, when Moses was grown that he went out unto his brethren, and looked on their burdens: and he spied an Egyptian smiting an Hebrew, one of his brethren. And he looked this way and that way, and when he saw that there was no man, he slew the Egyptian, and hid him in the sand, and when he went out the second day, behold, two men of the Hebrew strove together: and he said to him that did the wrong, wherefore smites thou thy fellow? And he said who made thee a prince and a judge over us? intendest thou to kill me as thou killedst the Egyptian? And Moses feared, and said, Surely this thing is known." Or as it is stated in the Amplified translation "One day after Moses was grown, it happened that he went out to his brethren and looked at their burdens; and he saw an Egyptian beating a Hebrew, one of Moses' brethren. He looked this way and that way, and when he saw no one, he killed the Egyptian and hid him in the sand. He went out the second day and saw two Hebrew men quarreling and fighting; and he said to the unjust aggressor, why are you striking your comrade? And the man said, who made you a prince and a judge over us? Do you intend to kill me, as you killed the

Egyptian? Then Moses was afraid, and thought, Surely this thing is known." In addition, Exodus 4:10 tells us that Moses was "slow in speech and of a slow tongue." However despite, being born in bondages, being abandoned as an infant, being endanger of death, being a murder, being rejected, being scorn, having difficulty in speaking and living as a fugitive he still led a life faithful to God and rose to the challenge God set for him. But Moses was not the only person who overcame challenges and lived a life faithful to God. The Bible teaches us in the 39th Chapter of The Book of Genesis that Joseph was so hated by his brothers that they conspired to kill him and after God intervened to spare his life his brothers sold him into slavery. Further that while in slavery he was accused of a crime he didn't commit and was cast into prison. However, despite suffering at the hands of his brothers who sought to kill and enslave him and being sent to prison for a crime he did not commit he still led a life of faithfulness towards God and God used him to save nations. The Bible teach us in the Book of Esther that even though Ester was orphaned and born into slavery, she still led a life of faithfulness towards God and God used her to marry a Persian King and save the Israelites from certain destruction. In addition, the 6-8 Chapter of the Book of Judges teaches us that Gideon who was born into poverty and oppression led a life of faithfulness towards God and God used him to deliver the nation of Israel from the oppression of the Midianites. Then there is David who was born into obscurity who was so insignificant to his family that when the Prophet Samuel was sent by God to the house of his father (Jessie) to anoint the King of Gods choosing Jessie not only failed to invite David to the sacrifice, but David was completely forgotten about by Jessie when it came time for Samuel to examine Jessie's sons to see who God had chosen King. However, despite being overlooked, devalued and neglected David lived a life of faithfulness towards God and became the greatest King Israel ever knew and was so pleasing to God that God described him as a man after his (God's) own heart. The Bible is full of stories of how ordinary men, and women and even children faced extraordinary challenges and setbacks, but through their faith in God found the strength to live lives of faithfulness towards God and allow God to use them to accomplish amazing feats for His glory. So whatever issues you may be facing whatever obstacles may be in your way do not allow them to become a hindrance to your living a life of faithfulness to God because whatever God is asking you for He has given you the gifts and abilities to do it and remember all things are possible to them who believe. In the 19th verse of the 25th Chapter of the Gospel according to Matthew, Jesus in teaching the parable about faithfulness declared "after a long time the Lord of those servants cometh, and reckoneth with them." This declaration raises two important points, the first is God provides us time to demonstrate our faithfulness and the second we will face an examination by God and must give an account. As it relates to the first point there a number of scriptures that teach us that our lives and our services to God is not Judged based on a single deed or activity, but rather over a measure of time. In the 9th verse of the 6th Chapter of the Book of Galatians the Apostle Paul while giving instruction on the value of Christian service admonished us when he said "And let us not be weary in well doing: for in due season we shall reap, if we faint not." And further instructed the church in 1 Cor. 15:58 "Be ye steadfast, unmovable, always abounding in the work of the Lord, forasmuch as ye know that your labor is not in vain in the Lord." Or as the Amplified translation states, " Therefore, my beloved, be firm (steadfast), immovable, always abounding in the work of the Lord—that is, always being superior (excelling, doing more than enough) in the service of the Lord, knowing and being continually aware that your labor in the Lord is not futile—never wasted or for no purpose." In these scriptures Paul was teaching the key to faithfulness, the consistent application of principles or the consistent adherence to the same practices over time, the key being the consistent application or adherence. Faithfulness is not determined by whether to submit to the will of God today, whether you pray today, whether we tithe today or even if we fail to do any of these things today, because faithfulness is not determined by the measure of our activity today, but rather the measure of our activity everyday.

In the 13th Chapter of the Gospel according to Matthew, Jesus in teaching the parable of the sower declared in verses 5-9 "some fell upon stony places, where they had not much earth: and forthwith they sprung up, because they had no deepness of earth: And when the sun was up, they were scorched; and because they had no root, they withered away. And some fell among thorns; and the thorns sprung up, and choked them: But other fell into good ground, and brought forth fruit, some a hundredfold, some sixty fold, some thirtyfold." In other words some showed great promise or perhaps performed well in the beginning, but when the test of time, trials, circumstance came their performance faded. Unfortunately many in the body of Christ seem to fall into this category. When they first hear the voice of God or feel a stirring in their spirit directing them to some service for God, they experience a great rush of excitement as images of immediate success or reward fill their minds and expectation of appreciation fill their hearts. However, as time progresses and those who they thought to be friends and supporters seem to vanish, personal financial dwindle or profession difficulties come or health issues develop their passion and commitment to the calling of God begins to dim. For others their once imaged approval turns to rejection or scorn and ridicule and the cost of their service to God begins to weigh them down or perhaps the demands on their schedule make continued service to God inconvenient. These are the ones that Jesus spoke of in Matthew 13: 5-7 each of whom appear to be faithful in the beginning, but all the cares of this world, the stress and strain of daily life seems to distract and consume them and cause them to fail the test of time.

As it relates to the second point and he "reckoneth with them" Jesus makes it clear that God requires us to answer for the work we have performed for him. The word reckoneth used in Matthew 25: 19 comes from the Greek word meaning to take an inventory. In other words when the appointing time had passed Jesus came to see what each of His servants had produced with what He had given them. It is important to note that the standard by which the three servants were Judged was not what they promised, but rather what they produced!

In Matthew 13: 8 while teaching the parable of the sower Jesus defines the "good ground" as the ground that "brought forth fruit" and in Matthew 7: 16-18 Jesus declared "Ye shall know them by their fruits. Do men gather grapes of thorns, or figs of thistles? Even so every good tree bringeth forth good fruit; but a corrupt tree bringeth forth evil fruit. A good tree cannot bring forth evil fruit, neither can a corrupt tree bring forth good fruit." Or as it is expressed in the Amplified Translation, " You will fully recognize them by their fruits. Do people pick grapes from thorns, or figs from thistles? Even so every healthy (sound) tree bears good fruit—worthy of admiration; but the sickly (decaying, worthless) tree bears bad and worthless fruit. A good (healthy) tree cannot bear bad (worthless) fruit, nor can a bad (diseased) tree bear excellent fruit—worthy of admiration. Even our professed intentions fail to satisfy the reckoning of Christ, for all our plans, promises and professed intentions as well as our excuses, justifications and misplaced priorities will not protect us from the truth of God's judgment. This fact is made clear in John 15. In the 15th Chapter of the Gospel according to John, Jesus teaching on the importance of our relationship with Him said "I am the vine, ye are the branches: he that abideth in me, and I in him, the same bringeth forth much fruit". In other words if we consistently adhere to the practices of Christ and consistently live by the principles of Christ, our faithfulness will produce fruit. I cannot emphasis the fact that a faithful life will produce fruit enough. Because a fruitful life is the true mark of a Christian (a follower of Christ) many in the church today are drawn by a religious experience, they are touched and inspired by the songs of praise, worship and faith. They are touched, inspired and filled with hope by sermons filled with stirring worlds which serve as reminders of God's love and promises of healing, redemption, forgiveness and blessings, but far too often there is not fruit. There is no fruit because there is not faithfulness, no faithfulness to the Commandment to love God, love our neighbor as we love ourselves, to feed the hungry, clothe the naked, comfort those in jail, visit those who are sick, be just to the fatherless, care for the widows, disciple the lost. I am sure that for many there is a desire for it to be done but a desire for it to be done is not the same thing as a commitment to do it, the commitment to consistently serve God by using the gifts abilities (talents) God has graciously given each of us, which is the essence of faithfulness, But for those who do have the desire to commit themselves to a life of service, a life of consistently making themselves available to God, God promises great reward. In Matthew 25: 21 and

23 respectively Jesus addresses those who have found to be faithful upon the Lord return and says "well done thou good and faithful servant: Thou hast been faithful over a few things, I will make thee ruler over many things: enter thou into the joy of the Lord". And in so doing offers the faithful servants acknowledgment, validation, recognition, promotion and joy. Of all the honors that the world hopes to offer, of all the offers of security the world hopes to provide, of all the riches and blessings a life in the world promises none can begin to compare to the knowledge that one is approved of by God. The world challenges us to create our own destinies to pursue riches and glory and to build dynasties for ourselves, but none of it will last because everything built of the flesh will fade. In the end it is only what we do for Christ which will last and only that which is born from our faithfulness which will be approved of by Him. Shouldn't it be the desire of everyone to please Him especially those who confess Him as Lord, shouldn't it be our goal, our desire, our passion to see those who are lost in sin to come to the knowledge of Christ.

3

THE LAW OF SOWING AND REAPING

The Law of Sowing and Reaping

The law of sowing and reaping states that the nature and magnitude of what we sow will determine the nature and magnitude of what we reap.

D. L. Wallace

While this law is taught throughout the Bible perhaps the clearest articulation of it is found in The 6th Chapter of the Book of Galatians in the 7th and 8th verses where the Apostle Paul teaching the Galatian church, admonished them to "Be not deceived; God is not mocked: For whatsoever a man soweth, that shall he also reap. For he that soweth to his flesh shall of his flesh reap corruption; but he that soweth to the spirit shall of the spirit reap life everlasting" or as the amplified translation of the Bible more clearly states "Do not be deceived and deluded and misled; God will not allow Himself to be sneered at –scorned, distained or mocked [by mere pretensions or professions, or His precepts being set aside]. He inevitably deludes himself who attempts to delude God. For whatever a man sows that and that only is what he will reap. For he who sows to his own flesh (lower nature, sensuality) will from the flesh reap decay and ruin and destruction, but he who sows to the spirit will from the spirit reap life eternal." Further, in the 9th Chapter of the second Book of Corinthians in the 6th verse the Apostle Paul admonished the church at Corinthians "But this I say, He which soweth sparingly shall reap also sparingly; and he which soweth bountifully shall reap also bountifully." Or as the Amplified translation of the Bible states "Remember this: he who sows sparingly and grudgingly will also reap sparingly and grudgingly, and he who sows generously and that blessing may come to someone, will also reap generously and with blessings." In other words the quality of your life is directly affected by what, why and how much you sow. I think it is evident from scripture that it is God's will that our lives be filled with goodness and it is not and has never been His intent that we experience corruption, however it is equally evident that God has provided each of us with instructions regarding how to live and has made the outcome of our lives dependent upon whether and the degree to which we abide by those instructions. In scripture as far back as the Book of Genesis God has expressed His intention, that His covenant people to be both blessed and be a blessing. In the 12th Chapter of the Book of Genesis verses 2 and 3 The Lord speaking to Abram declared. "And I will make of thee a great nation, and I will bless thee, and make thy name great; and thou shalt be a blessing: And I will bless them that bless thee and curse him that curseth thee: And in thee shall all families of the earth be blessed." Or as it is expressed in the Amplified translation of the Bible "and I will make of you a great nation, and I will bless you [with abundant increase of favors] and make your name famous and distinguished, and you shall be a blessing –dispensing good to others. And I will bless those who bless you [confer prosperity or happiness upon you], and curse him who curses or uses insolent language toward you; in you shall all the families and kindred of the earth be blessed-by you they shall bless themselves". In the 14th verse of the 3rd Chapter of the Book of Galatians the Apostle Paul makes it clear that the declarations made to Abraham by the Lord are made applicable to Christians through Jesus Christ when he state "that the blessings of Abraham might come on the Gentiles through Jesus Christ; that we might receive the promise of the spirit through faith." or as it is expressed in the Amplified translation "to the end that through [their receiving] Christ Jesus, the blessing [promised] to Abraham might come upon the Gentiles, so that we through faith might [all] receive [realization of] the promise of the (Holy) spirit." In other words that through receiving Jesus Christ by faith we might be made a great nation, be blessed, (with abundant increase of favors), have our name made famous and distinguished, we should be a blessing (dispensing good to others), and that through us all the families and kindred of the earth be blessed. In other words through our faith in Jesus Christ we should be blessed so that we can be a blessing or a dispenser of God, not just for the benefit of those in whom we sow but for our benefit as well., but what does it mean to sow? The word sow as it is used in the New Testament is derived from the Greek work speiro which means to scatter. When I think of the word sow in this context I get a picture of a farmer scattering seed in a manner which indicates his intention to cover the largest amount of territory and sow the greatest amount of seed as possible as oppose to one who plants by carefully placing in a particular location based on an presumption of the quality of the soil. I see an image of a farmer scattering seed generously based on the abundance of the seed possessed rather than sparingly being concerned about the condition of the soil.

In the 13th Chapter of the Gospel according to Matthew verses 3-8 Jesus teaching the parable of the sower illustrated the essence of a sower when He said "Behold, a sower went forth to sow; and when he sowed, some seeds fell by the way side, and the fowls came and devoured them up: Some fell upon stony places, where they had not much earth: and forthwith they sprung up, because they had no deepness of earth: and when the sun was up, they were scorched; and because they had no root, they withered away. And some fell among thorns; and the thorns sprung up, and choked them: But other fell into good ground, and brought forth fruit, some a hundredfold, some sixty fold, some thirtyfold". Further, the Amplified translation provides "And He told them many things in parables-that is, stories by way of illustration; saying,

A sower went out to sow, And as he sowed, some seeds fell by the roadside, and the birds came and ate them up. Other seeds fell on rocky ground, where they had not much soil, and at once they sprang up, because they had no depth of soil; But when the sun rose they were scorched, and because they had no root they dried up and withered away. Other seeds fell among thorns grew up and choked them out. Other seeds fell on good soil and yielded grain, some a hundred times as much as was sown, some sixty times as much, and some thirty". It is evident from this parable that the sower who serves as a type of Jesus and by extension a picture of us as we seek to fulfill God's will for our lives, was not calculating in his choice of locations of where to sow but rather was indiscriminatly sowing everywhere that was within his grasp. In order for us to understand the picture painted by Jesus in the parable of the sower there a few things we must understand. First the parable is about a sower and not simply a man who sows. This may appear to be a rather obvious fact not worthy of mention however I believe that there is more here than is first grasped. When Jesus described the character as a sower I believe that Jesus was speaking to his identity and his purpose. This was not someone who sowed occasionally or at moments of convenience but rather someone who "went forth to sow," someone who focused on the activity of sowing, someone who was consistent, committed and defined by sowing, someone who sowed with purpose. Second the sower was not moved by quick results. The parable tells us that his first attempt a sowing was met with failure ["and when he sowed, some seeds fell by the way side, and the fowls came and devoured them up") however his initial failure did not discourage him. The parable also tells us that his second attempt was met with limited and short term success ("some fell upon stony places, where they had not much earth: and forthwith they sprung up, because they had no deepness of earth") however, the sower did not stop sowing because it appeared he had positioned himself to receive a harvest nor did he stop to congratulate himself on his accomplishments. The third is that the sower was focused on the activity and not the harvest he would receive, which allowed the sower to continue sowing regardless of the immediate results. While it is evident from scripture that we will receive a harvest in connection with and in proportion to our sowing the Bible also teaches us that our harvest should not be our focal point. In the 6th Chapter of the Gospel according to Matthews verses 24-33 Jesus declared "No man can serve two masters: for either he will hate the one, and love the other; or else he will hold to the one, and despise the other. Ye cannot serve God and mammon. Therefore I say unto you, Take no thought for your life, what ye shall eat, or what ye shall drink; nor yet for your body, what shall ye put on. Is not the life more than meat, and the body than raiment? Behold the fowls of the air: for they sow not, neither do they reap, nor gather into barns; yet your heavenly Father feedeth them. Are ye not much better than they? Which of you by taking thought can add one cubit unto his stature? And why take ye thought for raiment? Consider the lilies of the field, how they grow; they toil not, neither do they spin: And yet I say unto you, that even Solomon in all his glory was not arrayed like one of these. Wherefore, if God so clothe the grass of the field, which today is, and tomorrow is cast into the oven, shall he not much more clothe you, O ye of little faith? Therefore take no thought, saying, what shall we eat? Or, what shall we drink? Or, Wherewithal shall we be clothed? (For after all these things do the Gentiles seek :) for your heavenly Father knoweth that ye have need of all these things. But seek ye first the kingdom of God, and his righteousness; and all these things shall be added unto you". Or as the Amplified translation states "No one can serve two masters; for either he will hate thee one and love the other, or he will stand by and be devoted to the one and despise and be against the other. You cannot serve God and mammon [that is, deceitful riches, money, possessions or "what is trusted in]. Therefore I tell you, stop being perpetually uneasy (anxious and worried) about your life, what you shall eat or what you shall drink, and about your body, what you shall put on. Is not life greater [in quality] than food, and the body [far above and more excellent] than clothing? Look at the birds of the air; they neither sow nor reap nor gather into barns, and yet your heavenly Father keeps feeding them. Are you not worth more than they? And which of you by worrying and being anxious can add one unit of measure [cubit] to his stature or to the span of his life?   And why should you be anxious about clothes? Consider the lilies of the field and learn thoroughly how they grow; they neither toil nor spin; Yet I tell you, even Solomon in all his magnificence (excellence, dignity and grace) was not arrayed like one of these. But if God so clothes the grass of the field, which today is alive and green and tomorrow is tossed into the furnace, will He not much more surely clothe you, O you men with little faith? Therefore do not worry and be anxious, saying, what are we going to have to eat? Or, what are we going to have to drink? or, what are we going to have to wear? For the Gentiles (heathen) wish for and crave and diligently seek after all these things; and your heavenly Father well knows that you need them all. But seek for (aim at and strive after) first of all His Kingdom and His righteousness [His way of doing and being right], and then all these things taken together will be given you besides." In other words, a sower cannot focus on what he shall reap (his blessings) but rather trust God to provide for him and focus his attention on sowing. The point is also made clear in the 6 verse of the 9th Chapter of the 2nd Book of Corinthians which states "[Remember] this: he who sows sparingly and grudgingly will also reap sparingly and grudgingly, and he who sows generously and that blessings may come to someone, will also reap generously and with blessing" (Amp) In other words the motivation of our sowing should be so "that blessings may come to someone" not ourselves or as it is expressed In the 9th and 10th verses of the 6th Chapter of the Book of Galatians where we are admonished "and let us not be weary in well doing: for in due season we shall reap, if we faint not. As we have therefore opportunity, let us do good unto all men, especially unto them who are of the household of faith." Or as expressed in the Amplified translation of the Bible "And let us not lose heart and grow weary and faint in acting nobly and doing right, for in due time and at the appointed season we shall reap, if we don't loosen and relax our courage and faint. So then, as occasion and opportunity open to us, let us do good (morally) to all people [not only being useful or profitable to them, but also doing what is for their spiritual good and advantage]. Be mindful to be a blessing, especially to those of the household of faith-those who belong to God's family with you, the believers." As I read the 9th and 10th verses of the 6th Chapter of the Book of Galatians I can imagine the frustration felt by the sower in Matthew 13 as he sows his seed only to see birds scoop down from the sky and devour it or as he watches seed which he has sown sprout up quickly and fill his heart with the promise of future gain, only to see his newly sprouted crops as well as his hopes die in the scorching heat or the seed which fell among the thorns as he watches the thorns spring up and choke his harvest . As I look at the Sower, I see a picture of so many in the body of Christ, whether in formal or lay ministry who have sown into the lives of others only to see their efforts fail to bare fruit in the lives into whom they have sown and I hear the spirit of the Lord encouraging them not to grow weary, dishearten or dismay because you will reap in due season, if you don't faint. Anyone who has spent anytime at all sowing in the lives of others knows how difficult it is, how often effort goes unnoticed, the heart break of seeing someone whom so much has been sown fall back into sin or bondage and while in moments like these it is easy to throw in the towel, remember God promised in Galatians 6:7 "you will reap what you sow." But He did not promise that you would reap where you sowed. In the 38th verse of the 6th Chapter of the Gospel according to Luke Jesus makes the connection between our sowing and our reaping abundantly clear when He state. "Give, and it shall be given unto you; good measure, pressed down, and shaken together, and running over, shall men give into your bosom. For with the same measure that ye mete withal it shall be measured to you again." Or as it is expressed in the Amplified translation of the Bible "Give, and [gifts] will be given you, good measure, pressed down, shaken together and running over will they pour into [the pouch formed by] the bosom [of your robe and used as a bag]. For with the measure you deal out-that is, with the measure you use when you confer benefits on other-it will be measured back to you." In order to fully understand the law of sowing and reaping we must understand the generosity of God and how we are called to be participants in His desire to use His generosity to change the world. In the 16th and 17th verse of the third Chapter of the Gospel according to John, Jesus makes a declaration which will both set the stage for and define everything the world will ever know about generosity when He said "for God so loved the world, that he gave his only begotten Son, that whosoever believeth in Him should not perish, but have everlasting life. For God sent not His son into the world to condemn the world; but that the world through him might be saved." Or as it is expressed in the Amplified "For God so greatly loved and dearly prized the world that He [even] gave up His only-begotten (unique) Son, so that whoever believes in (trusts, clings to, relies on) Him shall not perish-come to destruction, be lost-but have eternal (everlasting) life. For God did not send the Son into the world in order to judge—reject, to condemn, to pass sentence on-the world; but that the world might find salvation and be made safe and sound through Him. Just think about God's expression of generosity towards us that when the entire world was engulfed in sin having turned its back on God, having rejected centuries of overtures calling it to return and instead plunged deeper and deeper into the darkness God, who would have been just in destroying the world and forever blotting it out of His mind and eliminating any hope for redemption instead gave us the most valuable most precious gift of all, a gift so precious that even those of us who received Him cannot fully comprehend His true value. In light of this act which is the greatest act of generosity the world will ever know. Having received this gift how should we respond, should we having received this great gift commit our lives to ensuring all who God desires to receive it also have the opportunity to do so, or should we simply spend our time rejoicing in the gift given us knowing the certain peril that awakes those who die with out the opportunity that we rejoice for haven been given. This is the test we face the test of our true understanding of God's overwhelming generosity whether we who are so blessed to call Christ our Lord possess within our hearts the burden to share that gift with those who have not yet receive life through Him, this is why we sow. This is the test of true Christian maturity. The test of our true love for Christ and our desire to be like Christ is not demonstrated in our profession of our love for Him, but rather our willingness to surrender our time, our resources, our gifts, our lives to join Him in the mission for which He came, lived, bleed and died, the expression of God's love and the demonstration of God's true character through the surrender of His life so that those who God loved might live. This is the prerequisite for living a life as a sower a willingness, a desire to surrender our time, our resources, our gifts, our lives so that those who God loves might live.

In the 29th verse of the 8th Chapter of the Book of Romans the Apostle Paul speaking of the elect of God said "for whom he did foreknow, He also did predestinate to be conformed to the image of His son, that He might be the first born of many brethren" or as the Amplified translation says "for those whom He foreknew-of whom He was aware and loved beforehand-He also destined from the beginning (foreordaining them) to be molded into the image of His Son [and share inwardly His likeness], that He might become the first-born among may brethren." In other words before we were born we were chosen to be changed into someone who would possess and act out the nature of Jesus so that there would be many people on the earth who would act like Him. To act like Jesus is first and foremost to sow into the lives of those who are in need whether that need is physical, financial, emotional, relational, or spiritual. However, In order for us to be conformed to His image we must begin to see the world through the eyes and through the mind of Jesus. In the 1st and 2nd verses of the 12th Chapter of the Book of Romans the Apostle Paul admonished the church. "I beseech you therefore, brethren, by the mercies of God, that ye present your bodies a living sacrifice, holy, acceptable unto God, which is your reasonable service. And he not conformed to this world: but be ye transformed by the renewing of your mind, that ye may prove what is that good and acceptable, and perfect will of God." Or as the Amplified provides " I APPEAL to you therefore, brethren, and beg of you in view of [all] the mercies of God, to make a decisive dedication of your bodies-presenting all your members and faculties-as a living sacrifice, holy (devoted, consecrated) and well pleasing to God, which is your reasonable (rational, intelligent) service and spiritual worship. Do not be conformed to this world-this age, fashioned after and adapted to its external, superficial customs. But he transformed (changed) by the [entire] renewal of your mind-by its new ideals and its new attitude-so that you may prove [for yourselves] what is the good and acceptable and perfect will of God, even the things which is good and acceptable and perfect [in His sight for you]." In these scriptures the Apostle Paul expresses God's clear intentions that we as believes should, and I would argue, must reject the mind set of this world with its emphasis on selfishness, materialism, vanity, self-righteousness and self-absorption and instead take on the mind of Christ and with it the desire to live a life of service to those God loves, which is the essence of love. Throughout the Bible, especially in the Gospels God places a great emphasis on the need for service on the part of those who profess to love Him. In the 23rd and 24th verses of the 14th Chapter of the Gospel according to John, Jesus makes this point clear when He declared "If a man love me, he will keep my words: and my Father will love him, and we will come unto him, and make our abode with him. He that loveth me not keepeth not my sayings: and the word which ye hear is not mine, but the Father's which sent me." And the Amplified states "If a person [really] loves Me, he will keep my word-obey My teachings; and My Father will love him, and We will come to him and make Our home (abode, special dwelling place) with him. Anyone who does not [really] love Me does not observe and obey My teaching. And the teaching which you hear and heed is not Mine, but [comes] from the Father Who sent Me." And, in the 12th and 13th verse of the 15th Chapter of the Gospel according to John, Jesus declared "That ye love one another, as I have loved you. Greater love hath no man than this, that a man lay down his life for his friends." Or as the Amplified translation provides "This is My commandment, that you love one another [just] as I have loved you. No one has greater love-no one has shown stronger affection-than to lay down (give up) his own life for his friends." In other words we are commanded to love others as Jesus loves us, and the measure of that love does not lay in what we profess but what and to what degree and to whom we sow. In other words it is marked by our willingness to sow generously. Anyone with eyes and ears should be aware of the deteriorating condition of the world, the increase in the numbers of people who live in poverty, the increasing polarization of our society, the rise of drug use, suicide, the occult, the increasing pre-occupation with self, wealth and comfort often at the expense of those lease able to protect and provide for themselves. In the midst of all of this chaos, pain suffering, despair, hopeless many in the world are beginning to ask the question where is God. If God is loving, kind, forgiving, merciful where is He and why is He allowing this to occur? But I believe the better and more appropriate question is where are we, the church, those who profess to love and serve God? How did we allow darkness and suffering to spread into the lives of so many? Many would respond to my inquiry by pointing to the fact that the world does not live by the principles of God and as a result ungodliness produces suffering but I would suggest that the source of much of this is not the world but rather the ungodliness of some in the church. A church that in far too many instances has begun to act as the world's judge and not it's reconcilers, a church that has forgotten the promises God made to Abram and through Abram to us, that we will be a blessing and in us all the families of the earth shall be blessed. It is and has always been God's intention to use the church to stand in the position as Priest on behalf of those who have no relationship with God so that through our lives, our resources, our time, our gifts, our mercy, they would come to know the love of the invisible God through the actions of a visible people, a people who demonstrate the love of God to even those who do not have God in their life. This is the essence and focal point of sowing, to demonstrate love, both to those in whom we sow and to our Lord who sowed so much into us.

In verses 34 thru 40 of the 25th Chapter of the Gospel according to Matthew Jesus while teaching the parable of the talents said "Then shall the King say unto them on his right hand, Come, ye blessed of my Father, inherit the kingdom prepared for you from the foundation of the world: For I was an hungered, and ye gave me meat: I was thirsty, and ye gave me drink: I was a stranger, and ye took me in: Naked, and ye clothed me: I was sick, and ye visited me: I was in prison, and ye came unto me. Then shall the righteous answer him, saying, Lord, when saw we thee an hungered, and fed thee? Or thirsty, and gave thee drink? When saw we thee a stranger, and took thee in? Or naked, and clothed thee? Or when saw we thee sick, or in prison, and came unto thee? And the king shall answer and say unto them, Verily I say unto you, <u>Inasmuch as ye have done it unto one of the least of these my brethren, ye have done it unto me.</u>" Or as it is expressed in the Amplified translation "Then the King said to those at His right hand, Come, you blessed of My Father [that is, you favored of God and appointed to eternal salvation], inherit-receive as your own-the kingdom prepared for you from the foundation of the world. For I was hungry and you gave Me food; I was thirsty and you gave Me something to drink; I was a stranger and you brought Me with help and ministering care; I was in prison and you came to see Me. Then the just and upright will answer Him, Lord, when did we see You hungry and gave You food, or thirsty and gave You something to drink? And when did we see You a stranger and welcomed and entertained You, or naked and clothed You? And when did we see You sick or in prison and came to visit You? And the King will reply to them, Truly, I tell you, in as for as you did it to one of the least [in the estimation of men] of these My brethren, you did it to Me." In this scripture Jesus address three key points that need to be made clear if we are going to understand how to operate with the law of sowing and reaping. The first is into whom to sow. In the 25th Chapter of the Gospel according to Matthew Jesus set forth six categories of people those that are hungry, those who are thirsty, those who are alone, those that are naked, those that are imprisoned, and those who are sick each of which represent not only the natural condition of mankind but also the spiritual condition of those who do not know Jesus in the pardon of their sin as well as those who may know Jesus in the pardon of their sin but have yet to experience the power of Jesus in the deliverance and transformation of their lives and as a result are not living in the fullness of Christ. It is important to recognize that whether these categories are reviewed in their natural context, as a metaphor for a spiritual condition or both it is evident that they were in need.

This fact becomes important because so much attention is focused on sowing to get a harvest by sowing into those we presume are already blessed by God, that we run the risk of losing sight of those who need a blessing from God. However, in the text Jesus gave honor and reward to those who sowed into those in need. In addition, it is important that the scripture does not suggest that there was any natural relationship between those who sowed and those who received and in at least one case defined the recipient as a stranger. This becomes vital for a couple of reasons, the first is that the decision to sow into the life of another should be based upon a desire to do the will of God and not our desire to bless or provide for a particular person. While I am not suggesting that we should not strive to address the needs of certain people simply because we know them, I am suggesting that our desire to meet the needs of others should not be based on our personal relationship or lack thereof with them. Second our decision to sow should not be based on our expectation of receiving a direct or indirect benefit from the person into whom we have sown. It is often the case that when we sow into the lives of people with whom we have a personal relationship with we have an implicit if not explicit expectation of a reward in exchange, whether it is an offer of some form of influence in their lives, a well-timed express of public gratitude or other benefit. When this situation occurs, our motivates for sowing become impure and God is not honored because it is difficult for someone to recognize something as a gift from God if we have placed a price tag on the "gift". The second is that in each instance what was sown into the person was what they need to fix the issue that affected them. In the 18th verse of the 4th Chapter of the Gospel according to Luke when He declared "The spirit of the Lord is upon me, because He hath anointed me to preach the gospel to the poor; he hath sent me to heal the brokenhearted, to preach deliverance to the captives, and recovering of sight to the blind, to set at liberty them that are bruised." Or as it is expressed in the Amplified translation "The Spirit of the Lord [is] upon Me, because He has anointed Me [the Anointed One, the Messiah] to preach the good news (the Gospel) to the poor; He has sent Me to announce release to the captives, and recovery of sight to the blind; to send forth delivered those who are oppressed-who are downtrodden, bruised, crushed and broken down by calamity". In these scriptures we see that the operation of the Holy Spirit through Jesus resulted in Jesus sowing into the lines of each category of people exactly what they needed based on the specific needs of the people he would encounter. The third and final point is why they sowed.

Simply put they saw a need. It is evident from the scripture that there was no relationship between the people who sowed and those who received, it is also apparent from the text of the scripture that those who received the various blessings were not in the position to repay what was provided, there is no evidence in the scripture that any of those who received were of any particular religious position or moral character. In point of fact according to the scripture provides that one of them was a stranger so his position or moral character could not have been known and another was in jail and without any reference to his being a political prisoner or being persecuted for his commitment to his religious convictions in which case it is more likely than not he was in jail for the commission of a crime. For that matter it does not appear that there are any common denominator among them except one, each of them found themselves in need of something that they could not supply for themselves and in that regards they are like each of us, standing in a place of need that we cannot meet ourselves, praying that God will somehow meet it for us, waiting with great and sometimes disparate expectation that God will hear our prayer and lovingly and mercifully respond. The question is how, how does, God who is spirit respond to the needs of physical beings, can He respond to the needs of men without men who will allow God to use them?

In some instances He can, however in other instances it is not so simple. The Bible provides us with multiple examples where God moved supernaturally to provide for the needs of His people, However, in all but a few of them God enlisted the cooperation of a man whether it is God instructing Noah to construct the Ark or God using Moses to challenge Pharaoh for the destiny of the nation of Israel, to the old testament prophets used by God to bring the nation of Israel back to their first love, to new testament apostles, to modern day servants of God, God has clearly and continually expressed His intent to use man as His instrument on this earth. Some might raise the question why me? To which I would first respond why not you and then and perhaps more importantly I would respond because there is a need and the need is great. In fact I would submit to you that the only answer to the question is there is a need, why visit the sick, because there is a need, why feed the hungry or give shelter to the homeless, because there is a need, why care for the widows and the orphans there is a need the answer to every question about why you or I should serve Christ by serving others is because there is a need. But not only is there a great need, there is great opportunity. There is great opportunity to bring the light of Christ to those trapped in the darkness of sin, in hopelessness and despair, there is great need to show the love of Christ, to those who are lonely, have been abused, or suffer from neglect. There is a great opportunity to show the mercy of Christ to those who are afraid or who have fallen. There is great opportunity to show forgiveness to those trapped in sin, in guilt, or the peace of Christ to those who are confused, anxious, fearful and ignorant of God's promises concerning them. There is great opportunity to show the rest of Christ to those who are weary, overburden, overwhelmed struggling to make it through the next day, the next hour, the next minute, the next second. There is great opportunity to show the Power of Christ to a confused and sin sick world that is desperately trying to find peace, joy, fulfillment, happiness, success, value in everything but the one place where it can be found in Christ. Then there is the opportunity to show Jesus that we love Him and we are grateful for the mercy and grace that we discover a new with the rising of the sun each and everyday.

4

THE LAW OF TRANSFORMATION BY HEARING

The Law of Transformation by hearing

The law of transformation by hearing provides that what you hear today will determine what you will become tomorrow.

D.L. Wallace

In the 29th verse of the 8th Chapter of the Book of Romans, the Apostle Paul in writing to the believers in Roman speaking of God declared. "For whom he did foreknow, he also did predestinate to be conformed to the image of His Son, that he might be the firstborn among many brethren." Or as the Amplified translation states "For those whom He foreknew-of whom He was aware and loved beforehand-He also destined from the beginnings (foreordaining the) to be molded into the image of His Son [and share inwardly His likeness], that He might become the first-born among many brethren" thereby establishing God's clear intent that we be conformed into the image of Jesus so, that His inward likeness would be shown through us. The word conformed as it is used in this scripture is derived from the Greek word summorphos which means to be fashioned like unto and connotes the shaping of an object into the form of another. A view that is supported by the 12th Chapter of the Book of Romans the 2nd verse where the Apostle Paul wrote "and be not conformed to this world: but be ye transformed by the renewing of your mind, that ye may prove what is that good and acceptable, and perfect will of God." Or as it is expressed in the Amplified translation "Do not be conformed to this world-this age, fashioned after and adapted to its external, superficial customs. But be transformed (changed) by the [entire] renewal of your mind-by its new ideals and its new attitude-so that you may prove [for yourselves] what is the good and acceptable and perfect will of God, even the thing which is good and acceptable and perfect [in His sight for you]. I think that at this point it deserves mentioning that the good and acceptable and perfect will of God is for the likeness of Christ to be inwardly formed in us. The command expressed in 2nd verse of the 12th Chapter of the Book of Romans "be ye transformed by the renewing of your mind." Is both the hallmark and the benchmark of our relation with Christ and the bases of our hope in Him because anything other than the consistent and at times persistent transformation of our lives into the image of Christ is a false indicator of our salvation.

Many in the body of Christ have an earnest and heartfelt desire to live a life pleasing to God and to serve as an example for those around them that have not yet come to know Jesus as their Lord and Savior, but find that however earnest and heartfelt their desire they continually fall short of that desire. The result of this continual failure to realize their goal of living a Christ like life for many is a sense of powerlessness over their sins and shortcomings and a dampening of the fire of their faith which is justified by their personal experiences. For those who find themselves in this very painful situation it is important that they come to the realization that the source of their problem is not a lack of power, but rather a lack of knowledge, and as they struggle in their own power finding themselves falling in the category of those whom the Apostle Paul referred to in the 2nd verse of the 10th Chapter of the Book of Romans as those that are zealous for God, but their zeal is not based on knowledge." These are those who believe that obedience to God and the development of a Christ like character is a product of hard work and personal sacrifice which is in turn defendant upon the use of personal power to overcome the consequences of the carnal mind. It is sad to say those who pursue righteousness through their own efforts (works) will never find it and will deny themselves what is perhaps the greatest blessing available to a Christian a changed heart which comes from a renewed mind, because only a mind renewed in Christ Jesus can change a human heart and only a changed heart can result in changed behavior. In the 5th through 8th verses of the 8th Chapter of the Book of Romans the Apostle Paul declared "for they that are after the flesh do mind the things of the flesh; but they that are after the spirit the things of the spirit. For to be carnally minded is death; but to be spiritually minded is life and peace. Because the carnal mind is enmity against God: for it is not subject to the law of God, neither indeed can be. So then they that are in the flesh cannot please God." Or as the Amplified translation expresses it "For those who are according to the flesh and controlled by its unholy desires, set their minds on and pursue those things which gratify the flesh. But those who are according to the spirit and [controlled by the desires] of the spirit, set their minds on and seek those things which gratify the (Holy) spirit. Now the mind of the flesh [which is sense and reason without the Holy Spirit] is death-death that comprises all the miseries arising from sin, both here and hereafter. But the mind of the (Holy) spirit is life and soul peace [both now and forever]. [that is] because the mind of the flesh with its carnal thoughts and purposes- is hostile to God; for it does not submit itself to God's law, indeed it cannot. So then those who are living the life of the flesh – catering to the appetites and impulses of their carnal nature – cannot please or satisfy God, or be acceptable to Him." Therefore, those who continue to operate with their natural mind or continue to think with their natural mind cannot live a life pleasing to God and sadly will not understand just how far from living a life pleasing to God their life really is. In the 15th verse of the 16th Chapter of the Gospel according to Luke Jesus spoke on the consequences of living a life based on the natural mind when. He declared" Ye are they which justify yourselves before men; but God knows your hearts: For that which is highly esteemed among men is abomination in the sight of God." Or as the Amplified states "You are they who declare, yourselves just and upright before men, But God knows your hearts. For what is exalted and highly thought of among men is detestable and abhorrent (abomination) in the sight of God." This plight that Jesus referred to in Luke 16:15 is the consequence of man attempting to be righteous based on the perceptions of the carnal (natural) mind. What is often missed by those who face this dilemma is that it is often not our will that drives our behavior, but our understanding. Even those with the greatest desire to do what is right make choices based on what they understand to be true, what they understand to be right, what they understand to be necessary, and even what they understand to be God's will and as a result even the most well intended person can live a life contrary to God's will, if they don't understand God's true nature or have an accurate understanding of God's will.

The History of the Church is full of examples of well-intended men and women who committed grave and often tragic error in an attempt to fulfill what they mistakenly believed to be God's will. One such example is the Prophet Samuel. The 16th Chapter of the 15th Book of Samuel recounts the story of God's selection of David as the second King of Israel after the tragic fall of King Saul. In the first verse of 1 Samuel 16 God directs the Prophet Samuel to go to the house of Jessie the Bethlehemite because God had chosen a King from his sons. However, when Samuel arrived something interesting transpired. In verses 6-7 of the 16th Chapter of the 1st Book of Samuel the Bible declares "And it came to pass, when they were come, that he looked on Eliab, and said, Surely the Lord's anointed is before him. But the Lord said unto Samuel, Look not on his countenance, or on the height of his stature; because I have refused him: for the Lord seeth not as man seeth; for man looketh on the outward appearance, but the Lord looketh on the heart." Or as the Amplified states "When they had come, he looked on Eliab [the eldest son], and said, surely the Lord's anointed is before Him. But the Lord said to Samuel, Look not on his appearance or at the height of his stature, for I have rejected him; for the Lord sees not as man sees; for man looks on the outward appearance, but the Lord looks on the heart. In this passage of scripture God draws a very stark distinction between the standards of man as compared to the standards of God and highlights the danger and the potential for even those with the best intentions to error when they attempt to make decisions based on the natural mind. It is evident from scripture that Samuel was a man who loved God and desired to please Him. The Bible teaches us that Samuel was born do to the direct and miraculous intervention of God in response to his mother (Hanna's) pleas for mercy; that he was dedicated to God as an infant and was raised in the temple under the care and instruction of the Chief Priest Eli. However, yet in still Samuel when operating in His natural mind could not accurately discern the will of God relating to God's choice of a King to replace King Saul and in an effort to obey the will of God sought to offer God something that while acceptable to him, was displeasing to God. Another example of the dangers of operating in our natural minds is found in the story of Saul of Tarsus. Saul of Tarsus, who is more commonly and graciously known to us as the Apostle Paul, like the Prophet Samuel Saul of Tarsus had a quite impressive background in the religious traditions and standing of his day. In the 5th and 6th verses of the 3rd Chapter of the Books Philippians the Apostle Paul in describing his religious pedigree described himself as "Circumcised the eighth day, of the stock of Israel, of the tribe of Benjamin, an Hebrew of the Hebrews; as touching the law, a Pharisee; Concerning zeal, persecuting the church; touching the righteousness which is in the law, blameless. However, despite all of his religious training, despite his commitment to honor God and to live his life not only according to God's will but in God's service he found himself not only missing God's will for the salvation and deliverance of Israel but actively and I might add zealously opposing it to the point of dedicating himself to destroying the very Church that God, (in the person of Jesus) came to establish. The Bible is full of stories of men and women who unknowingly found themselves opposing the will of God. While in each case the factual circumstances are different the underlying factor is the same, the reliance on the natural mind as the basis of their decisions, because as the Apostle Paul wrote in the 7th verse of the 8th Chapter of the Book of Romans. "The carnal mind is enmity against God: for it is not subject to the law of God, neither indeed can be." Or as the Amplified translation so accurately states "[that is] because the mind of the flesh- with its carnal thoughts and purposes- is hostile to God; for it does not submit itself to God's Law, indeed it cannot." In each of these cases the party in question, whether it is the Prophet Samuel, the Apostle Paul or any of the other men or women of God who inadvertently found themselves on the wrong side of God's will there is one common denominator, a mind operating based on human or carnal understanding. Human understanding that, as it always does, fails to discern or understand God's will. This is because we in our natural capacity are incapable of understanding much less thinking like God. In the 7th through 9th verses of the 55th Chapter of the Book of Isaiah, God declared "Let the wicked forsake his way, and the unrighteous man his thoughts; and let him return unto the Lord, and he will have mercy upon him; and to our God, for he will abundantly pardon. For my thoughts are not your thoughts, neither are your ways my ways, saith the Lord. For as the heavens are higher than the earth, so are my ways higher than your ways, and my thoughts than your thoughts." When God declared that His thoughts were higher than our thoughts and His ways were higher than our ways it becomes clear that God sees the world and our lives differently than we do, God who is in possession of all knowledge and all power recognized possibilities that are not only far greater than those we could possible imagine, but also knows the true facts, causes, and effects of every situation and as a result makes the perfect decision for every intended outcome. As a result God's desire for good demands our absolute obedience to His will and His commands and any failure to adhere to His instructions is not only disobedience, but also results in far reaching consequences that, we may never realize in this life time. Further, while we are often not aware of them, God is and it is these often unrecognized consequences that God's instructions are intended to prevent. God realizing that the natural mind is enmity with Him and produces decisions and activities contrary to His will set forth a plan to change man's condition. God's plan begins with our call to repentance, but true repentance is more than a mere apology and desire to escape divine punishment or to prevent earthly consequences, resulting from our actions. It is a change of our beliefs, opinions, emotions and mental state or at least a heartfelt and mental desire to do so. In short repentance is an acknowledgment of our error and willingness to change. Our need to change or be transformed is the hallmark of our relationship with Christ and the bedrock of the Christian experience, but the question is how do we as Christians change or should I say how are we transformed. The short answer is through our hearing. If it is true as we stated earlier that God judges the heart, "Then merely adopting specific behavior with no accompanying change of heart fails to satisfy the command of God expressed through the Apostle Paul in the 2nd verse of the 12th Chapter of the Book of Romans where he declared "and be not conformed to this world: but be ye transformed by the renewal of your mind, that ye may prove what is that good, and acceptable, and perfect, will of God." Or as it is expressed in the Amplified translation "Do not be conformed to this world-this age, fashioned after and adapted to its external, superficial customs. Be transformed (changed) by the [entire] renewal of your mind-by its new ideals and its new attitude – so that you may prove [for yourselves] what is the good, and acceptable and perfect will of God, even the thing which is good and acceptable and perfect [in His sight for your]" In other words you can change who you are by changing what you think.

The 7th verse of the 23rd Proverb teaches us that "For as He thinketh in his heart so is he" in other words the product of our mind is produced in our lives and therefore our thought life or our thought processes become key in determining how much, if any, of the life God has for us we will receive or even recognize. In the 9th through 14th verses of the 2nd Chapter of the 1st Book of Corinthians the Apostle Paul address the consequences and limitations of operating with the natural mind while attempting to deal with the things of God when he wrote "But as it is written, eye hath not seen, nor ear heard, neither have entered into the heart of man, the things which God hath prepared for them that love Him. But God hath revealed them to us by His spirit: for the spirit searcheth all things, yea, the deep things of God, for what man knoweth the things of a man, save the spirit of man which is in him? Even so the things of God knoweth no man, but the spirit of God. Now we have received, not the spirit of the world, but the spirit which is of God; that we might know the things that are freely given to us of God, which things also we speak not in the words which man's wisdom teacheth, but which the Holy Ghost teacheth; comparing spiritual things with spiritual. But the natural man receiveth not the things of the spirit of God: for they are foolish unto him: neither can he know them, because they are spiritually discerned." Or as the Amplified translation explains "But, on the contrary, as the Scripture says, What eye has not seen, and ear has not heard, and has not entered into the heart of man, [all that,] God has prepared-made and keeps ready-for those who love Him [that is, for those who hold Him in affectionate reverence, promptly obeying Him and gratefully recognizing the benefits He has bestowed]. Yet to us God has unveiled and revealed them by and through His Spirit, for the (Holy) Spirit searches diligently, exploring and examining everything, even sounding the profound and bottomless things of God-the divine counsels and things hidden and beyond man's scrutiny. For what person perceives (knows and understands) what passes through a man's own spirit within him? Just so no on discerns (comes to know and comprehend) the thoughts of God except the Spirit of God. Now we have not received the spirit (that belongs to) the world, but the (Holy) Spirit Who is from God, [given to us] that we might realize and comprehend and appreciate the gifts (of divine favor and blessing so freely and lavishly) bestowed on us by God. And we are setting these truths forth in words not taught by human wisdom but taught by the (Holy) Spirit, combing and interpreting spiritual truths with spiritual language [to those who possess the (Holy) Spirit]. But the natural, non-spiritual man does not accept or welcome or admit into his heart the gifts and teachings and revelations of the Spirit of God, for they are folly (meaningless nonsense) to him; and he is incapable of knowing them-of progressively recognizing, understanding and becoming better acquainted with them-because they are spiritually discerned and estimate and appreciated." As we read and more importantly consider this scripture something very clear and I hope thought provoking emerges that we must choose to live our lives and by extension define our future either by the thoughts of man or by the thoughts of God. The unfortunate reality is that the necessity of this choice is often overlooked or at least under emphasized by many in the Body of Christ. In fact many in the Body of Christ continue to cling to many of the ideals, opinions, desires and expectations they possessed or should I say that possessed them prior to their becoming saved. With many of those who fall in this category, living completely unaware of the command to renew their minds, seek to understand God's word from the vantage point of human logic and human wisdom and as a result disconnect or even worse completely disregard any command of God which does not fit neatly within the confines of their worldly expectations. Other still are so committed to their notations of human logic and human reasoning that they place limitations on God based on what they believe is fair, reasonably, appropriate, practical, or possible that they in effect create, in their own mind, a God of such limited power and such limited authority that God becomes (in their view) a God unable to heal, bless, restore, prosper or protect and the examples in scripture where God did each of these things simply become stories or metaphors or perhaps fables as opposes to examples of fulfilled promises upon which to build their faith. Tragically, I believe that these people are those that Jesus referred to in the parable of the sower where the seed fell by the way side.

In the 15th verse of the 4th Chapter of the Gospel according to Mark, Jesus while teaching the parable of the sower explained "and these are they by the way side, where the word is sown; but when they have heard, Satan cometh immediately, and taketh away the word that was sown in their hearts" they hear the word but the word has no effect in their lives, because it does not produce any change in their mind. I believe that people who fall into this category are also those that Jesus was addressing in the 13th through 15th verses of the 13th Chapter of the Gospel according to Matthew when He declared "Therefore speak I to them in parables: because they seeing see not; and hearing they hear not, neither do they understand. And in them is fulfilled the Prophecy of Esaias, which saith, By hearing ye shall hear, and shall not understand; and seeing ye shall see and shall not perceive: For this people's heart is waxed gross, and their ears are dull of hearing, and their eyes they have closed; lest at anytime they should see with, their eyes, and hear with their ears, and should understand with their heart, and should be converted, and I should heal them." Or as the Amplified translates "This is the reason that I speak to them in parables, because having the power of seeing they do not see, and having the power of hearing they do not hear, nor do they grasp and understand. In them indeed is the process of fulfillment of the Prophecy of Isaiah which says: You shall indeed hear and hear, but never grasp and understand; and you shall indeed look and look, but never see and perceive.

For this nation's heart has grown gross-fat and dull; and their ears heavy and difficult of hearing, and their eyes they have tightly closed, lest they see and perceive with their eyes, and hear and comprehend the sense with their ears, and grasp and understand with their heart, and turn and I should heal them." Others still seem to operate under a dual mindset, part anchored in the wisdom and logic of the world and part struggling to live under the influence of the word of God. Those who fall in this category readily recognize the power and Authority of God and His ability and perhaps His willingness to heal, deliver, restore, protect, and even prosper. However, they still see value in the wisdom of the world. For them God is one of a number of options and God's plan serves as one of a number of alternatives that they have the ability and even the right to choose from depending on whether a particular provision of God's word suits them or whether God's word "makes sense" to them based on the circumstance they encounter or the goals or objectives they are pursuing. Often times they see themselves committed to all or at least a portion of God's will but not necessarily committed to God's way; believing instead that they can accomplish the will of God while operating in the world ways. As a result they produce for themselves a hybrid Christianity which focuses on the theoretical will of God, but with little taste or attitude for the practical application of His will. However, despite how common place this position may be in the Body of Christ the Bible issues a clear warning to those who desire to operate in the Kingdom and the world, based on their belief in the world's wisdom more than the wisdom of the word. In the 6TH through 8th verses of the 1st Chapter of the Book of James the Bible warns "But let him ask in faith, nothing wavering. For he that wavereth is like a wave of the sea driven with the wind and tossed. For let not that man think that he shall receive any thing of the Lord. A double minded man is unstable in all his ways." Or as the Amplified translation provides "Only it must be in faith that he asks, with no wavering-no hesitating, no doubting. For the one who wavers (hesitates, doubts) is like the billowing surge out at sea, that is blown hither and thither and tossed by the wind. For truly, let not such a person imagine that he will receive anything [he is] unstable and unreliable and uncertain about everything he thinks, feels, decides). In addition Jesus spoke directly against this double-mindedness in the 24th verse of the 6th Chapter of the Gospel according to Matthew when He declared. "No man can serve two masters: For either he will hate the one, and love the other; or else he will hold to the one, and despise the other. Ye cannot serve God and mammon." Or as it is expressed in the Amplified translation "No one can serve two masters; either he will hate the one and love the other or he will stand by and be devoted to the one and despise and be against the other. You cannot serve God and mammon [that is deceitful riches, money, possessions, or what is trusted in].

It is unfortunate that those in the Body who find themselves attempting to operate with both spiritual and carnal mindsets more often than not find themselves consumed by the world and as a result fail to fulfill God's will for their lives, I believe these are the people Jesus spoke of In 16th through 19th verses of the 4th Chapter of the Gospel according to Mark when He said "and these are they likewise which are sown on stony ground; who, when they have heard the word, immediately receive it with gladness; and have no root in themselves, and so endure but for a time: afterward, when affliction or persecutions ariseth for the word's sake, immediately they are offended. And these are they which are sown among thorns; such as hear the word and the cares of this world. And the deceitfulness of riches, and the lusts of other things entering in, choke the word, and it becometh unfruitful. Or as the Amplified states "And in the same way the ones sown upon stony ground are those who, when they hear the Word, at once receive and accept and welcome it with joy. And they have no real root in themselves, and so they endure for a little while, then when trouble or persecution arises on account of the Word, they immediately are offended-because displeased, indignant, resentful; and they stumble and fall away. And the ones sown among the thorns are others who hear the Word, Then the cares and anxieties of the world, and distractions of the age, and the pleasure and delight and false glamour and deceitfulness of riches, and the craving and passionate desire for other things creep in and choke and suffocate the Word, and it becomes fruitless." In other words their carnal mindedness with its fleshly expectations, perceived limitations, adherence to human reasoning and logic serve to render the word of God void and fruitless in their lives, this fact is tragic not only because of the impact it has on the lives of those who chose to continue to be carnal minded but also in light of the effect it has on so many others whose lives will never be impacted by them the way God intended. That is why it is vitally important that as Christians we are always mindful that the decisions we make not only affect us and our families but also untold numbers of people many of whom we may never come to know. Just image if Abram having heard the voice of the Lord refused instead choose to remain with His family. Or if Moses having heard God command him to go tell Pharaoh to let the nation of Israel go, believed more in the power of Pharaoh than the power of God and chose instead to remain in the wilderness. Think of the lives that would have been adversely affected by their decision to operate in their carnal minds. So then what do we do, how do we who, were born into and shaped by a world system produced and operated by a mindset which is often directly opposed to the will and ways and perhaps the very existence of God, manage to free ourselves from its grip? The answer is found in the word of God. In the 2nd verse of the 12th Chapter of the Book of Romans, the Apostle Paul admonishes us "And be not conformed to this world: but be ye transformed by the renewing of your mind, that ye may prove what is that good, and acceptable and perfect will of God" Or as the Amplified states "Do not be conformed to this world-this age, fashioned after and adapted to its external, superficial customs. But be transformed (changed) by the [entire] renewal of your mind- by its new ideals and its new attitude-so that you may prove [for yourselves] what is the good and acceptable and perfect will of God, even the things which is good and acceptable and perfect [in His sight for you]." In examining Romans 12: 2 there are a number of things which become apparent. The first is whether we are conformed or transformed is our choice and it is a choice that each of us must make. While it is true that all of us were born into a world whose belief and views oppose the will and perhaps even the existence of God, it is also true that when we receive Jesus Christ as our Lord and Savior we are no longer bound to our past. In fact the Apostle Paul makes this abundantly clear in the 17th verse of the 5th Chapter of the 2nd Book of Corinthians when he declared "Therefore if any man be in Christ, he is a new creature: old things are passed away; behold, all things become new." Or as the Amplified translation states "therefore, if any person is (engrafted) in Christ, the Messiah, he is (a new creature altogether,) a new creation; the old (previous moral and spiritual condition) has passed away. Behold, the fresh and new has come!" In other words while we may look like the person we were before we came to Christ we are an entirely different person, and that person unlike the person we use to be has the power, and I would argue the obligation, to choose to be transformed through the renewing of our minds. Further, it is important to recognize that our power to choose arises not from the power of our will but rater from the power of Christ who now dwells with us. Because while we in our flesh are weak to sin greater is He, (Jesus) that is in us than he (satan) who is in the world and as the Apostle Paul declared in the 37th verse of the 8th Chapter of the Book of Romans "In all these things we are more than Conquerors through Him who loves us" Or as Amplified translation states "Yet amid all these things we are more than conquerors and gain surpassing victory through Him who loves us."

Second we must recognize that the values of this world along with its goals, standards, beliefs, customs and ways of doing things must not be our source of truth, identity, purpose, or desire. In the 15th and 16th verses of the 2nd Chapter of the 1st Book of John, The Apostle John warning of the growing tendency of carnality in the church wrote '"Love not the world, neither the things that are in the world. If any man loves this world, the love of the Father is not in him. For all that is in the world, the lust of the flesh, and the lust of the eyes, and the pride of life, is not of the Father, but is of the world. Or as the Amplified translations provides "Do not love or cherish the world or the things that are in the world. If anyone loves the world, love for the Father is not in him. For all that is in the world the lust of the flesh [craving for sensual gratification] and the lust of the eyes [greedy longings of the mind], and the pride of life [assurance in one's own resources or in the stability of earthly things] – these do not come from the Father but are from the world [itself]." Or as the Apostle James declared in the 4th verse of the 4th Chapter of the Book of James "Ye adulterers and adulteresses, know ye not that Friendship of the world is enmity with God? Whosoever therefore will be, a friend of the world is the enemy of God." Or as the amplified translation states "You [are like] unfaithful wives [having illicit love affairs with the world] and breaking your marriage vow to God! Do you not know that being the world's friend is being God's enemy? So whoever chooses to be a friend of the world takes his stand as an enemy of God." I cannot state this point clearly enough until we reject and even denounce the values, goals, standard's, beliefs, customs and ways of doing things of this world we will not be open to receiving the values, goals, standards, beliefs, customs and ways of doing things from God.

Third in order for us to be transformed by the renewing of our minds we must draw our new ideas and our new attitudes from the word of God. If it is true as the Bible declares in the 7th verse of the 23 Proverb that "As a man thinketh in his heart, so is he" And if it is true as the Apostle Paul declared in the 29th verse of the 8th Chapter of the Book of Romans that "For who he did foreknow, he also did predestinate to be conformed to the image of his Son, that He might the first born among many brethren" or as the amplified explains "For those whom He foreknew-of whom He was aware and loved before hand-He also destined from the beginnings (fore-ordaining them) to be molded into the image of His son [and share inwardly His likeness], that He might become the first-born among many brethren's." Then not only must we accept new ideas and new attitudes, but they must be His ideas and attitudes.

In the 1st Chapter of the Book of Joshua God spoke to Joshua the newly appointed leader of the nation of Israel to prepare him for the transformation to a people of promise and in the 8th verse declares "This Book of the law shall not depart out of thy mount; but thou shalt meditate therein day and night, that thou may observe to do according to all that is written therein: for then thou shalt make thy way prosperous, and thou shall have good success." Or as the Amplified provides "This Book of the law shall not depart out of your mouth, but you shall meditate on it day and night, that you may observe and do according to all that is written in it; for them you shall make your way prosperous and then you shall deal wisely and have good success." In other words we are to speak and think about Gods word constantly. I think that it is evident to everyone that the key to learning is repetition and that what we hear most often is what we are most likely to believe to be true. We see evidence of this in almost every area of our lives. Think of the way we learn the words to the music we listen to or the lines from the commercials we hear day in and day out before long we know every line without any conscious effort. Now think about how often we believe information is true simply because we have heard it repeatedly. The reason for this is simple we learn from repetition or more specifically from hearing information repeatedly. This fact is borne out in scripture in the 17th verse of the 10th Chapter of the Book of Romans the Apostle Paul declared "Faith cometh by hearing, and hearing by the word of God." Or as the Amplified states so faith comes by hearing [what is told], and what is heard comes by the preaching [of the message that came from the lips] of Christ, the Messiah [himself]. "In other words when we hear the word of God, we hear Christ speak. It is this word of God spoken unto us by Christ Himself, often through human agents and other times by the spirit of God Himself, that serves as the weapon of our transformation because as we hear the word of God, it shatters every Stronghold, casts down every imagination and pulls down every high thing that exalts itself against the knowledge of Christ and brings every thought to the obedience of Christ. As a result, as we hear the word of God we are transformed by hearing until not only are we transformed by the word of God but we are transformed into the word of God.

5

THE LAW OF FORGIVENESS

The Law of Forgiveness

The Law of forgiveness states: The measure of forgiveness we receive will be determined by the measure we give.

D.L.Wallace

Forgiveness for many is the most difficult of all of the Commandments that Jesus gave to His disciples because it strikes right at the core of our basic (carnal) need to survive. It also strikes at the core of our need for revenge which is a perversion of our sense of justice as well as our prideful sense of self-righteousness. On the other hand the willingness to forgive is one of the foundational elements of our Christ likeness. As I considered the Law of Forgiveness it became evident how the law of forgiveness like many of the spiritual laws that affect our lives operate on the principle of reciprocal grace.

In the 14th and 15th verses of the 6th Chapter of the Gospel according to Matthew Jesus while instructing the disciples how to pray declared "For if ye forgive men their trespasses, your heavenly Father will also forgive you: But if ye forgive not men their trespasses, neither will your Father forgive your trespasses." Or as the Amplified states "For if you forgive people their trespasses-that is, their reckless and willful sins, leaving them, letting them go and giving up resentment-your Father will also forgive you. But if you do not forgive others their trespasses – their reckless and willful sins, leaving them, letting them go and giving up resentment – neither will your Father forgive you your trespasses." And in the 37th verse of the 6th Chapter of the Gospel according to Luke Jesus declared "Judge not, and ye shall not be Judged: Condemn not, and ye shall not be condemned: Forgive, and ye shall be forgiven." Or as it is expressed in the Amplified "Judge not- neither pronouncing judgment or subjecting to censure-and you will not be judged; do not condemn and pronounced guilty, and you will not be condemned and pronounced guilty; acquit and forgive and release (give up resentment, let it drop), and you will be acquitted and forgiven and released." In both these passages Jesus sets forth the law of forgiveness. However despite the clear Biblical mandate to forgive, forgiveness is perhaps one of if not the most difficult of the Christian virtues to master. At its core, forgiveness is an expression of pure and unconditional love a whole hearted desire that the one to whom we extend forgiveness have a life free of suffering, pain and judgment regardless of the wrong they have done and more specifically done to us. In the 4th through 8th verses of the 13th Chapter of the 1st Book of Corinthians in teaching on the nature of Love the Apostle Paul declared. "Charity suffereth long, and is kind; charity envieth not; charity vaunteth not itself, is not puffed up, Doth not behave itself unseemly, seeketh not her own, is not easily provoked, thinketh no evil; Rejoiceth in the truth, Beareth all things, believeth all things, hopeth all things, endureth all things. Charity never faileth: but whether there be prophecies, they shall fail, whether there be tongues, they shall cease; whether there be knowledge, it shall vanish away. Or as it is expressed in the Amplified "Love endures long and is patient and kind; love never is envious nor bails over with jealousy; is not boastful or vainglorious, does not display itself haughtily. It is not conceited – arrogant and inflated with pride; it is not rude (unmannerly), and does not act unbecomingly. Love [God's love in us] does not insist on its own rights or its own way, for it is not self-seeking; it is not touchy or fretful or resentful; it takes no account of the evil done to it – pays no attention to a suffered wrong. It does not rejoice at injustice and unrighteousness, but rejoices when right and truth prevail. Love bears up under anything and everything that comes is ever ready to believe the best of every person, its hopes are fadeless under all circumstances and it endures everything [without weakening]. Love never fails – never fades out or becomes obsolete or comes to an end." This is a picture of forgiveness and as Jesus teaches us in Matthew 6:14-15 as well as Luke 6: 37 as we forgive others God will forgive us. This willingness to grant forgiveness is an act of mercy which is to be given to others not based on how they behave or even how remorseful they are for the things they have done or failed to do, but because of who we are in God or at least who we recognize we should be in Him.

However if we are to begin, or for that matter continue, to walk in forgiveness there are a few things we are going to have to recognize and come to terms with.

The first of which is our pride. Pride is an inflated sense of value or entitlement which results from a belief in one's goodness or importance apart from Christ and is rooted in an illusion of self-righteousness. In verses 1 through 11 of the 8th Chapter of the Gospel according to John the Bible teaches us an important lesson on forgiveness. In the verses 1 through 11 John tell of the woman caught in adultery and provides "Jesus went unto the mount of olives. And early in the morning he came again into the temple, and the people came unto him; and he sat down, and taught them. And the scribes and Pharisees brought unto him a woman taken in adultery; and when they had set her in the midst, they say unto him, Master, this woman was taken in adultery, in the very act. Now Moses in the law commanded us, that such should be stoned: but what sayest thou? This they said, tempting him that they might have to accuse him. But Jesus stooped down, and with his finger wrote on the ground, as though he heard them not. So when they continued asking him, he lifted up himself, and said unto them, He that is without sin among you, let him first cast a stone at her. And again he stooped down, and wrote on the ground. And they which heard it, being convicted by one, beginning at the eldest, even unto the last and Jesus was left alone, and the woman standing in the midst. When Jesus had lifted up himself, and saw none but the woman, he said unto her, Women, where are those thine accusers? Hath no man condemned thee? She said, No man, Lord. And Jesus said unto her, neither do I condemn thee: go, and sin no more." Or as the Amplified translation sets forth "But Jesus went to the Mount of Olives. Early in the morning (at dawn), He came back into the temple court and the people came to Him in crowds. He sat down and was teaching them, when the Scribes and Pharisees brought a woman who had been caught in adultery. They made her stand in the middle of the court and put the case before Him teacher, they said, this woman has been caught in the very act of adultery. Now Moses in the law commanded us that such [women, offenders] shall be stoned to death but what do you say [to do with her]? – What is your sentence? This they said to try (test) Him, hoping they might find a charge for which to accuse Him. But Jesus stooped down and wrote on the ground with His finger. However, when they persisted with their question, He raised Himself up and said, let him who is without sin among you be the first to throw a stone at her. Then He bent down and went on writing on the ground with His finger. They listened to Him and then they began going out conscience-stricken one by one, from the oldest down to the last one of them, till Jesus was left alone with the woman standing there before Him in the center of the court. When Jesus raised up He said to her, Woman, where are your accusers? Has no man condemned you? She answered, no one, Lord! And Jesus said, I do not condemn you either. Go on your way, and from now on sin no more." In considering the story of the women caught in adultery there are several points that are worth mentioning. The first is the prideful condition of the Scribes and the Pharisees. Anyone who is familiar with the History of the Bible will recognize that the Pharisees and Scribes positioned themselves as the authority on the meaning of the word of God and presumed for themselves the right to ostracize and even condemned anyone who sought to challenge their interpretation of the word of God, I believe it is note worthy that their primary purpose for bring this woman to the temple was not to seek justice for the offense she committed but rather to test Jesus by seeking to determine whether He would pass judgment in a manner that was right in their eyes or whether Jesus himself should be condemned. What many of us fail to realize is that our failure to forgive is in essence a judgment or condemnation on God. When we refuse to forgive someone we are telling God that He has no right to extend mercy to them and His (God's) decision to be merciful is itself unjust. We also tell God that we have the right to exercise judgment on His children that is independent and contrary to His. However, few people who find themselves in this situation recognize this fact and many will argue that it is untrue because the truth of our hard heartiness and our self-righteousness is masked behind our assertion that the offending person is guilty of the offense. In the 4th and 5th verses of the 8th Chapter of the Gospel according to John, the Pharisees and the Scribes proclaimed "this woman had been caught in the very act of adultery. Now Moses in the law commanded us that such [women, offender] should be stoned to death." In other words she is guilty and we just want justice, or as it is more often expressed "do you know what they did"? Thereby attempting to use her sin to mask their true spiritual condition, it is amazing just how often we seek to use the behavior of others to mask our own selfishness, hard heartedness and hatred as if our attempts to conceal it from man will mask it from God. As I read this passage of scripture I found it truly ironic that those who presumed to represent God sought to use God's word to condemn God for His desire to show mercy. I wonder how many times we have found ourselves in the position of using God's word to hinder God's will because the nature of our heart blinds us to the heart of God., how many times we as the Pharisees and Scribes did in this text filter God's word through hatred and pride and find ourselves opposing people who are in the same spiritual condition that we are asking God to bring judgment upon them while at the same time asking God to spare us from judgment. Yes they were right, she had sinned but at the risk of appearing unkind or unsympathetic to their cause or for that matter to ours if she or in our case they had not committed the offense or if no harm was done there would be no need of forgiveness.

The second is that the Pharisees and Scribes were so consumed with their position as enforcers of the laws of God that they could not recognize the activity of God. In the 2nd and 3rd verses of the 8th Chapter of the Gospel according to John the Bible declares "Early in the morning (at dawn), He came back into the temple court and the people came to Him in crowds. He sat down and was teaching them, when the Scribes and Pharisees brought a woman who had been caught in adultery. They made her stand in the middle of the court and put the case before Him." (AMP) here we see Jesus the Son of God, the Christ, the Messiah sitting in the temple of God, drawing a crowd of people to Him teaching them the word of God and in so doing teaching them to live a life that honors God by focusing on the will of God. Here is Jesus carrying out the ministry of reconciliation drawing men unto Him and then a group of Pharisees and Scribes come into the temple and interrupt Jesus, disrupt His class, His ministry attempting to discredit Him and accuse Him by seeking to force Jesus in a position of either drawing people to God or using the law to condemn the woman. I believe that there are many times were we are faced with the choice of reconciling someone to God or condemning them based on the law with realizing the choice we must make. It is interesting to note that the Pharisees and the Scribes entire purpose (God ordained) was to cause people to return to God and in so doing remove the curses that caused Israel to suffer at the hands of the Romans and the Greeks before them, however their self-righteous behavior served to have the opposite effect, by attempting to focus attention on man's desire for judgment as oppose to God's desire for forgiveness. It cannot be stated clearly enough that unforgiveness and the spirit of condemnation that results serve only to disrupt and hinder true reconciliation.

The third is that the Pharisees and Scribes became so consumed with the illusion of self-righteousness and the faults of others that they could no longer see themselves. In verses 7 through 9 of the 8th the Chapter of the Gospel according to John the Bible states "However, when they persisted with their questions, He raised Himself up and said, let him who is without sin among you be the first to throw a stone at her. Then He bent down and went on writing on the ground with His finger. They listened to Him and then they began going out conscience-stricken one by one, till Jesus was left alone with the woman standing there before Him in the center of the court." (AMP) I find it very interesting how the Pharisees and the Scribes were so caught up in the sins of the woman they were accusing they had forgotten their own. It is even more amazing to me how much we are like them. So very often when we are harm or mistreated we cry out for "justice", or perhaps a better word for it is revenge, we expect that God, will see the unspeakable harm that has be fallen us, the social injustices that so offend our enlightened conscience and morality while at the same time believing that God has a blind eye to the sins we have committed or the harm we have caused, pretending as the Pharisees and Scribes in this story to stand sinless before God, righteous in our own right. But what if as the scripture suggests only the sinless had a right to condemn, only the innocent to cry out for justice, how would that effect our cause. What if as is at least implicitly suggested God will either Judge all, (for all have sinned and fallen short of the glory of God) or forgive all regardless of our self-serving perceptions of degrees of sin or degrees of harm. In reading the text I am confident that the Pharisees and Scribes who brought the woman to Jesus were convinced that her sins were so great that Jesus would have no choice but to side with them and agree to their judgment that she was not entitled to God's mercy and as a result Jesus would not interfere with their decision to cancel her destiny and become the instrument of her demise or risk sharing her fate. Isn't it interesting how when we stand in unforgiveness towards someone it is not enough that we seek to punish them by denying them mercy, but we expect everyone else to punish them as well and we seek to punish those who, show mercy to those we seek to punish. But look at how their confidence in their self-righteousness faded when Jesus took the focus off the woman being accused and focused it on those who presumed themselves to be righteous enough to accuse her. Notice that Jesus did not accuse them, even though Jesus who is and was God in the flesh knew all of their sins and failures, but rather prompted them to examine themselves. I find it amazing Jesus did not accuse them and does not accuse us, but yet they as well as we believe that our accusations are inspired by God.

In the 1st through 5th verses of the 7th Chapter of the Book of Matthew Jesus spoke directly to this issue when He declared "JUDGE NOT, that ye be not judged. For with what judgment ye judge, ye shall be judged: and with what measure ye mete, it shall be measured to you again. And why beholdest thou the mote that is in thy brother's eye, but considereth not the beam that is in thine own eye? Or how wilt thou say to thy brother, Let me pull out the mote out of thine eye; and behold, a beam is in thine own eye? Thou hypocrite, first cast out the beam of thine own eye; and then shalt thou see clearly to cast out the mote out of thy brother's eye." Or as it is expressed in the Amplified translation "DO NOT judge and criticize and condemn others, so that you may not be judged and criticized and condemned yourselves. For just as you judge and criticize and condemn others you will be judged and criticized and condemned, and in accordance with the measure you deal out to others it will be dealt out again to you. Why do you stare from without at the very small particle that is in your brother's eye, but do not become aware of and consider the beam of timber that is in your own eye? Or how can you say to your brother, Let me get the tiny particle out of your eye, but do not become aware of and consider the beam of timber that is in your own eye? You hypocrite, first get the beam of timber out of your own eye, and then you will see clearly to take the tiny particle out of your brother's eye." I realize that for some in the body of Christ this scripture seems to be unrelated to the issue of forgiveness especially in circumstances where you have suffered or have been subjected to harm from someone you do not know or to whom you have done no harm. In situations like these it is natural to look at the circumstance in terms of the events that transpired and from that vantage point the issue of fault is clear. However, let me remind you that if it is only in situations where wrong have occurred that forgiveness is required. When we as Christians experience hurt or harm it is important that instead of asking whether the person that harmed us deserves forgiveness we should instead ask whether God requires us to forgive them and whether or not we have or will ever need forgiveness. I believe that by shifting our focus away from the injury we have suffered and shifting it towards God's plan for reconciliation not only between us and them, but more importantly between us and God we will be better able to understand our circumstances from God's point of view and understand how our willingness to forgive is linked to our Godlikeness.

In addition to the issue of pride, we must also address the issue of fear. It is often the case that when we suffer pain or loss at the hands of someone that one of the greatest obstacles to our willingness to forgive is fear. Fear that we will be seen as weak, fear we will leave ourselves unprotected and fear that if we offer forgiveness the person that caused our suffering or loss will repeat the behavior and will hurt us again. However, if we are going to be able to learn to operate in forgiveness as God requires we must put the issue of fear in its proper Biblical context. First, in the 7th verse of the 1st Chapter of the II Book of Timothy the Apostle Paul declares "For God hath not given us the spirit of fear; but of power, and of love and of a sound mind". Or as the Amplified translation states "For God did not give us a spirit of timidity – cowardice, of craven and cringing and fawning fear- but [He has given us a spirit] of power and of love and of calm and well-balanced mind and discipline and self-control." In this scripture the Apostle Paul make it clear that fear is not of God, but rather God gives us the spirit of power and of love and of a sound mind. In addition in the 18th verse of the 4th Chapter of the 1st Book of John the Apostle John speaking on love declared "there is no fear in love; but perfect love casteth out fear: because fear hath torment. He that fearth is not made perfect in love." Or as it is expressed in the Amplified translation "There is no fear in love-dread does not exist; but full-grown (complete, perfect) love turns fear out of doors and expels every trace of terror! For fear brings with it the thought of punishment, and [so] he who is afraid has not reached the full maturity of love-is not yet grown into love's complete perfection." In other words the fear that we feel has as its basis our incomplete understanding and acceptance of God's love and as a result we fear punishment from God. In the 28th verse of the 8th Chapter of the Book of Romans the Apostle Paul declared "And we know that all things work together for good to them that love God, to them who are called according to his purpose." Or as the Amplified states "We are assured and know that [God being a partner in their labor], all things work together and are [fitting into a plan] for good to those who love God and are Called according to [His] design and purpose." In other words God uses everything that happens in our lives for our good. However, as long as we question the magnitude of God's love towards us it will be difficult to have the confidence to stand in this truth and not fear that those who we are required to forgive will do us harm. In addition, the story of Joseph sheds a great deal of light on this subject. The story of Joseph is a story of betrayal, persecution and victory. In the beginning of the story we see Joseph, Jacob's favorite son, being kidnapped by his brothers and sold into slavery only to find himself the victim of false accusations and cast in jail. Imagine the pain and sorrow Joseph felt having been betrayed by his own brothers, brothers so jealous of him that they planned his murder and after realizing that they could not kill him, threw him into a pit stole his coat, which was a symbol of his father's love and sold him like cattle. Imagine how he felt as he was taken to a slave market and resold to an Egyptian. Surround by strangers, stripped of his home, his father, his culture and sentenced to a life of servitude. Just think how easy it would have been for Joseph to allow the pain of his betrayal to turn to bitterness. Just imagine what must have been racing through his mind as he served his Egyptian masters day after day as the number of days he went without experiences his father love grew. Further imagine his time in prison, accused of a crime he did not commit jailed on the word of a man whose house and honor he sought to protect, the insult to his character, the blemish upon his name. However, in the midst of all of this Joseph never forgot the vision God have him and never lost his faith in God. As the story of tells us Joseph found favor with Pharaoh Servants and was ultimately brought before Pharaoh to interpret a dream and by interpreting the dream of Pharaoh gained position and favor. It is Joseph position that results in Joseph's brothers, the same brothers who betrayed him and sold him into slavery coming before him in need of his mercy. In the 16th through 21st verses of the 50th Chapter of the Book of Genesis the Bible tells the story of their reunion and says "And they sent a messenger unto Joseph, saying, thy father did command before he died, saying, so shall ye say unto Joseph, Forgive, I pray thee now, the trespass of thy brethren, and their sin; for they did unto thee evil: and now, we pray thee, forgive the trespass of the servants of the God of thy father. And Joseph wept when they spake unto him. And his brethren also went and fell down before his face; and they said, behold, we be thy servants and Joseph said unto them, fear not: for am I in the place of God? But as for you, ye thought evil against me; but God meant it unto good, to bring to pass, as it is this day, to save much people alive. Now therefore fear ye not: I will nourish you, and your little ones. And he comforted them, and spake kindly unto them." Or as the Amplified states "And they sent a messenger to Joseph, saying, your father commanded before he died, saying, so shall you say to Joseph, Forgive [take up and away all resentment and all claim to requital] I pray you now, concerning the trespass of your brothers and their sin; for they did evil to you. Now, we pray you, forgive the trespass of the servants of your father's God. And Joseph wept when they thus spoke to him. Then his brothers went and fell down before him, saying, See, we are your servants-your slaves! And Joseph said to them, Fear not; for am I in the place of God? [Vengeance is His, not mine.] As for you, you thought evil against me; but God meant it for good, to bring about that many people should be kept alive, as they are this day. Now therefore do not be afraid. I will provide for and support you and your little ones. And he comforted them [imparting cheer, hope, strength], and spoke to their hearts [kindly]. It is evident from the readying of this scripture that Joseph realized what the Apostle Paul taught us in the 28th verse of the 8th Chapter of the Book of Romans "that all things work together for good to them that love God, to them who are called according to his purpose." Whenever I read the story of Joseph, like so many of the men and women of God who stand confidently in the love of God in the most painful times of their lives I can hear them saying what the prophet Isaiah declared in the 17th verse of the 54th Chapter of the Book of Isaiah when he declared the prophetic word of God "No weapon that is formed against thee shall prosper; and every tongue that shall rise against thee in judgment thou shall condemn. This is the heritage of the servants of the Lord, and their righteousness is of me, saith the Lord." Or as the amplified states "But no weapon that is formed against you shall prosper, and every tongue that shall rise against you in judgment you shall show to be in the wrong. This [peace, righteousness, security, triumph over opposition] is the heritage of the servants of the Lord [those in whom the ideal Servant of the Lord is reproduced]. This is the righteousness or the vindication which they obtain from

Me-this is that which I impart to them as their justification- says the Lord." Once we come to understand that the protection of God is more than sufficient then we can arrive at a place where our forgiveness will not be hindered by fear. The third thing we are going to have to deal with, if we are going to fulfill God's mandate for forgiveness is our desire for revenge. For some in the body of Christ the greatest hindrance for forgiving those who have injured as is a desire for revenge. The desire that those who have injured us or caused us harm, should themselves suffer harm. In fact many would argue that this is not a desire for revenge but rather a desire for justice; however that is simply not true. The reason that many believe that justice results in the punishment of the offender rather than restoration for the injured party is because we often confuse our desire to seek revenge with God's right to vengeance because only God has a right to vengeance, because it is God's law or commandment that was broken not ours. In the 19th verse of the 50th Chapter of the Book of Genesis, Joseph in addressing his brothers fear that Joseph might seek revenge for the wrong they had done to him spoke directly to this issue. The Bible declares "And Joseph said unto them, Fear not: For am I in the place of God?" Or as the Amplified translation states "And Joseph said to them, Fear not; For am I in the place of God?

[Vengeance is His, not mine]." In this scripture Joseph responds to his brother's fear that he might seek revenge by asking an interesting question that I believe everyone who struggles with the desire for revenge should ask themselves "Am I in the place of God" because only God has a right to vengeance. In the 18th verse of the 19th Chapter of the Book of Leviticus Moses while giving the nation of Israel instructions on how to deal with their neighbors stated "Thou shalt not avenge, nor bear any grudge against the children of thy people, but thou shalt love thy neighbor as thyself: I am the Lord." Or as it is expressed in the Amplified translation "You shall not take revenge or bear any grudge against the sons of your people, but you shall love your neighbor as yourself. I am the Lord." This scripture leaves no room for debate that it is God and not mankind who has the right to seek revenge. In the 35th verse of the 32nd Chapter of Deuteronomy God through His servant Moses declared "To me belongeth vengeance, and recompense; their foot shall slide in due time: for the day of their calamity is at hand, and the things that shall come upon them make haste." Or as the Amplified translation states "Vengeance is Mine, and recompense, for the time when their foot shall slide; for the day of their disaster is at hand, and their doom comes speedily." Perhaps the Apostle Paul said it best. In the 16th through 21st verses of the 12 Chapter of the Book of Romans the Apostle Paul declared "Be of the same mind one toward another. Mind not high things, but condescend to men of low estate. Be not wise in your own conceits. Recompense to no man evil for evil. Provide things honest in the sight of all men. If it be possible, as much as lieth in you, live peaceably with all men. Dearly beloved, avenge not yourselves, but rather give place unto wrath: for it written, Vengeance is mine; I will repay, saith the Lord. Therefore if thine enemy hunger, feed him; if he thirst, give him drink: for in so doing thou shalt heap coals of fire on his head. Be not overcome of evil, but overcome evil with good." Or as the Amplified translation states "Live in harmony with one another; do not be haughty (snobbish, high minded, exclusive), but readily adjust yourself to [people, things] and give yourselves to humble tasks. Never overestimate yourself or be wise in your own conceits. Repay no one evil for evil, but take thought for what is honest and proper and noble-aiming to be above reproach-in the sight of every one. If possible, as far as it depends on you, live at peace with everyone. Beloved, never avenge yourselves, but leave the way open for [God's] wrath; for it is written, Vengeance is Mine, I will repay (requite), says the Lord. But, if your enemy is hungry, feed him; if he is thirsty, give him drink;

for by so doing you will heap burning coals upon his head. Do not let yourself be overcome by evil, but overcome (master) evil with good." Let me reiterate that "Live in harmony with one another; do not be haughty (snobbish, high minded, exclusive, but readily adjust yourself to estimate yourself or be wise in your own conceits. Repay no one evil for evil, but take thought for what is honest and proper and noble-aiming to be above reproach-in the sight of everyone. If possible, as far as it depends on you, live at peace with everyone. Beloved, never avenge yourselves, but leave the way open for [God's] wrath; for it is written, Vengeance is Mine, I will repay (requite), says the Lord. But, if your enemy is hungry, feed him; if he is thirsty, give him drink; for by so doing you will heap burning coals upon his head. Do not let yourself be overcome by evil, but overcome (master) evil with good. In other words trust God to fight your battles and forgive. Because when it is all said and done it all comes down to the question do we trust God, or maybe I should ask how much do we trust God. Because until we learn to trust God as our protector and stand in confidence in the fact that the Battle is not ours but the Lords we will never have the power to forgive and will continue to have un-forgiveness and malice in our hearts toward those God requires us to forgive. When we hold un-forgiveness in our hearts we seldom realize the harm that we do to ourselves and to our destinies. Un-forgiveness produces hatred, wrath, strife, variance, seditions, envying and sometimes murder which constitutes works of the flesh (Gal 5: 20-21) which will hinder God's activity in our lives. Further having these works of the flesh in our hearts can result in them becoming seed sown into our lives and the lives of others. In the 45th verse of the 6th Chapter of the Gospel according to Luke Jesus concerning the content of our hearts when He declared "a good man out of the good treasure of his heart bringeth forth that which is good; and an evil man out of the evil treasure of his heart bringeth forth that which is evil: For of the abundance of the heart his mouth speaketh." Or as the Amplified translations states "The upright (honorable, intrinsically good) man out of the good treasure [stored] in his heart produces what is upright (honorable intrinsically good); and the evil man out of the evil storehouse brings forth that which is depraved (wicked and intrinsically evil), for out of the abundance (overflow) of the heart his mouth speaks." This is one of the reasons why forgiveness is so important and un-forgiveness is so dangerous. The more we refuse to forgive the more we hold on to and store up the anger, pain and resentment that the original offense or offenses produce and overtime, they produce a toxic bitterness that poison the heart. Un-forgiveness operates much like cancer perverting the heart by killing the love, mercy, tenderness and goodness produced by a healthy heart until the heart is no longer a source of good and becomes a source of evil. That is why I believe the warning contained in the 21st verse of the 12th Chapter of the Book of Romans "Be not overcome of evil, but overcome evil with good." The key to overcome evil with good is found in our willingness to forgive or as the Apostle Paul instructed us in the 20th verse of the 12th Chapter of the Book of Romans "Therefore if thine enemy hunger, feed him; if he thirst, give him drink: for in so doing thou shalt heap coals of fire on his head." As we commit to operate in forgiveness we prevent the pain and suffering caused by others from hardening our hearts which in turns prevents us from sowing into the flesh which in turn allows us to avoid reaping a harvest of death and instead allows us to reap life which is part of our destiny in Jesus Christ. In the 7th and 8th verses of the 6th Chapter of the Book of Galatians the Apostle Paul warned "Be not deceived; God is not mocked: For whatsoever a man soweth, that shall he also reap. For he that soweth to his flesh shall of the flesh reap corruption; but he that soweth to the spirit shall of the spirit reap life everlasting." Do not be deceived and deluded and misled; God will not allow Himself to be sneered at scorned, disdained or mocked [by mere pretensions or professions, or His precepts being set aside] – He inevitably deludes himself who attempts to delude God. For whatever a man sows, that and that only is what he will reap. For he who sows to his own flesh (lower nature, sensuality) will from the flesh reap decay and ruin and destruction; but he who sows to the spirit will from the spirit reap life eternal." [Amp] In other words regardless of our reasoning, our justifications or our statements to the contrary if we sow anger, bitterness, strife, un-forgiveness and the like we will reap destruction in our lives, which is clearly not God's will for His children, which is one of the reasons why God gave us the command to forgive. Forgiveness allows us to become more like God. In the 16th and 17th verse of the 9 Chapter of the Book of Nehemiah the prophet Ezra In describing the nation of Israel's relationship with God wrote "But they and our fathers dealt proudly, and hardened their necks, and hearkened not to thy commandments, And refused to obey, neither were mindful of thy wonders that thou didst among them; but hardened their necks, and in their rebellion appointed a captain to return to their bondage: but thou art a God ready to pardon, gracious and merciful, slow to anger, and of great kindness, and forsooketh them not." Or as the Amplified provides "But they and our fathers acted presumptuously and stiffened their necks, and did not heed Your commandments; They refused to obey, nor were they mindful of Your wonders and miracles which You did among them; but stiffened their necks, and in their rebellion appointed a captain that they might return to their bondage [in Egypt]. But You are a God ready to pardon, gracious and merciful, slow to anger, and of great steadfast love, and You did not forsake them." Or as the Psalmist wrote in the 5th verse of the 86th Psalm "For thou, Lord, art good, and ready to forgive; and plenteous in mercy unto all them that call upon thee." Or as it is expressed in the Amplified translation "For You, O Lord, are good, and ready to forgive [our trespasses]-sending them away, letting them go completely and forever; and You are abundant in mercy and loving-kindness to all those who call upon You." Furthermore, given God's nature is that of one who is so eager to forgive, despite our flaws and sinfulness how much more should, we who so desperately need His forgiveness have a willingness to forgive. How can we dare to claim to be like Christ who came into this world to provide forgiveness for all, who forgave the very ones who crucified Him at the foot of the vary cross upon which He hung and yet not forgive those who have offended us. Just think about the power of forgiveness as a means of opening a door for us to bear witness to the love of Christ; how our very act of forgiveness can show those who have offended or injured us the power of Christ's love as it is shown through us. But perhaps most importantly our willingness to forgive is key to our receiving the forgiveness we need in order to continue on our journey towards becoming the men and women God pre-ordained us to be. While it has been stated before it is well worth repeating that the measure of forgiveness we receive will be determined by the measure of forgiveness we give.

6

THE LAW OF THANKSGIVING

The Law of Thanksgiving

The Law of Thanksgiving provides that the degree to which we create an atmosphere of Thanksgiving is the degree to which we will experience His presence.

D.L. Wallace

In the 4th verse of the 100th Psalm the psalmist "wrote Enter into His gates with thanksgiving, and into His courts with praise: be thankful unto him, and bless His name." Or as the Amplified translation provides "Enter into His gates with thanksgiving and with a thanks offering, and into His courts with praise: Be thankful and say so to Him, bless and affectionately praise His name." The word thanksgiving as it used in the 4th verse of the 100th Psalm comes from the Hebrew word "Towdah" which means an extension of the hand in adoration and connotes an offering or expression of thanks. Thanksgivings in its simplest form is an offering or expression of gratitude to God in response to God's activity and therefore, should be distinguished from an offering of praise. While the distinction between thanksgiving and praise and for that matter worship is lost on many in the church, the distinctions are not lost on God. In point of fact I believe that one of the reasons the church as a whole is not experiencing the power of God as God intended is we have lost sight of the importance of these distractions and as a result marred our offerings to God. In that regard there are a couple of things that the 4th verse of the 100th Psalms has to teach us.

The first is that there is a proper order for entering into God's presence. The 4th verse of the 100th Psalm declares "Enter into His gates with thanksgiving." The bible teaches us that the temple was divided into three sections or courts the outer court, the inner court, and the holies of holies and that surrounding the temple was a wall and that the wall contained thirteen Gates. The purpose of the wall was to protect the temple from intruders or those who desired to enter into the temple for improper purposes and grant entry only to those who entered lawfully through on of the gates. Therefore, we can only enter into the temple through gates and we can only enter into the gates with thanksgiving. It is our thanksgiving that sets us apart from the rest of the world. The second is that we cannot enter into His courts until we have entered into his gates. This may seem overly simplistic to some, but the importance of this fact cannot be overstated because we cannot truly praise God for who He is until we first become thankful for what He does. God is a spirit and as such has no physical form to look upon, no hands to feel, no smile to behold, no body to embrace and God's thoughts cannot be understood beyond what He chooses to reveal and how He choose to reveal them.

It is evident throughout scripture, that the principle means by which God reveals His thoughts to us is through His activity and therefore as we learn what He does, we learn and come to appreciate His nature. However the unfortunate truth is that there are many, even many in the church who experience God's activity everyday, but still do not recognize that it is God, much less offer Him thanksgiving for it. Many of who believe that they are the masters of their own fate and the source of their own blessings all the while being deceived into an idolatress worship of themselves or their possessions having unknowingly been seduced by the satanic rulers of this age and in far too many instances having sold their souls for their thirty pieces of silver. Some do this not realizing that by so doing they are pushing themselves further and further away from the God who loves them, being consumed by their own pride. For what man looking at the vastness of space, the amazing force of the sun, the diversity of the creatures that inhabit the earth could help but acknowledge the power, goodness and generosity of God. What man seeing all God created could help, but stand in a position of thankfulness to God.

King David in verses 1-3 of the 24th Psalm declared "The earth is the Lord's and the fullness thereof; the world, and they that dwell therein. For he hath founded it upon the seas, and established it upon the floods. Who shall ascend into the hills of the Lord? Or who shall stand in His holy place? Or as the Amplified translation provides "The earth is the Lord's, and the fullness of it, the world and they who dwell in it. For He has founded it upon the seas, and established it upon the currents and the rivers. Who shall go up into the mountains of the Lord? Or who shall stand in His holy place? "In those verses of scripture David acknowledges God as not only the source, but the owner of all things. This acknowledgment that God is the creator and owner of all things including mankind is the prerequisite of developing an attitude of thanksgiving because if we truly recognize that as the Bible teaches us that God created the heaven and the earth and that God is the rightful owner of it all then it is a natural extension of the realization of that truth to recognize that everything we have or every blessing we experience is because of God. Or as the Psalmist declared in the 1st through 14th verses of the 50th Chapter Psalm when he wrote "The mighty God, even the Lord, hath spoken, and called the earth from the rising of the sun unto the going down thereof. Out of Zion, the perfection of beauty, God hath shined. Our God shall come, and shall not keep silence; a fire shall devour before him, and it shall be very tempestuous round about him. He shall call to the heavens from above and the earth, that He may judge His people. Gather my saints together unto me; those that have made a covenant with me by sacrifice. And the heavens shall declare his righteousness. For God is judge himself. Selah. Hear o my people, and I will speak O Israel, and I will testify against thee: I am God, even thy God I will not reprove thee for thy sacrifices or thy burnt offering, to have been continually before me. I will take no bullock out of thy house, nor he goats out of the folds. For every beast of the forest is mine, and the cattle upon a thousand hills. I know all the fowls of the mountains: and the wild beast of thy field are mine. If I were hungry, I would not tell thee: For the world is mine, and the fullness thereof. Will I eat the flesh of bulls, or drink the blood of goats? Offer unto God thanksgiving; and pay thy vows unto the most High." Or as the Amplified translation declares "The mighty one, God the lord, speaks and calls the earth from the rising of the sun to its setting, out of Zion, the perfection of beauty, God shines forth, Our God comes, and does not keep silence; a fire devours before him, and round about Him almighty tempest rages. He calls to the heavens above and to the earth, that He may judge His people: Gather together to me my saints [those who have found grace in my sight], those who have made a covenant with me by sacrifice. And the heavens declared His righteousness –rightness and justice; for God, He is judge. Selah. [Pause, and calmly think of that]. Hear, O my people, and I will speak; O Israel, I will testify to you and against you; I am God, your God. I do not reprove you for your sacrifices; your burnt offerings are continually before me.

I will accept no bull form your house, nor he-goat out of your folds. For every beast of the forest is mine and the cattle upon a thousand hills or upon the mountains where thousands are. I know and am acquainted with all the birds of the mountains, and the wild animals of the field are mine and are with me, in my mind. If I were hungry, I would not tell you, for the world and its fullness are mine. Shall I eat of the flesh of bulls, or drink the blood of goats? Offer to God the sacrifice of thanksgiving; and pay your vows to the most High." In this scripture God speaking through the Psalmist speaks directly to the appropriateness of our offering of thanksgiving as well as its importance as an entry point in our having right relationship with God. In these 14 verses God asserts his sovereignty as He describes how God speaks and calls the earth from the rising of the sun to its setting. Making it clear to all of those who will listen, that He and He alone has the right to command the movements and activities upon the earth and the right to judge His people. That God and God alone establishes righteousness and order upon the earth. God further explains the need for us to soberly consider the rightness and purity of His sovereignty and His method of expressing it because it is based upon our response to it that we will be judged. As the Psalm unfolds we are faced with the sobering possibility that our actions towards God may not be approved but rather rejected by Him because our actions offend rather than Honor Him. This potential of offending God is not solely based upon our actions, but the expression of the content of our heart behind them. As we examine this text we must most assuredly examine our lives to make sure that which we offer to God is in fact acceptable to Him for what value is there in providing an offering to God if the manner in which it is offered so pollutes the item offered to God that it rendered the offering unacceptable to Him. In the first nine verses of the first Chapter of the Book of Leviticus the Bible declares "And the Lord called unto Moses, and spake unto him out of the tabernacle of the congregation; saying, speak unto the children of Israel, and say unto them, if any man of you bring an offering unto the Lord, ye shall bring your offering of the cattle, even of the herd, and of the flock. If his offering be a burnt sacrifice of the herd, let him offer a male without blemish: he shall offer it of his own voluntary will at the door of the tabernacle of the congregation before the Lord. And he shall put his hand upon the head of the burnt offering; and it shall be accepted for him to make atonement for him. And he shall kill the bullock before the Lord: And the Priests, Aaron's sons, shall bring the blood round about upon the alter that is by the door of the tabernacle of the congregation.

And he shall flay the burnt offering and cut it into his pieces. And the sons of Aaron the Priest shall put fire upon the altar, and lay the wood in order upon the fire; And the Priest, Aaron's sons, shall lay the parts, the head, and the fat, in order upon the wood that is on the fire which is upon the altar: But his inward and his legs shall burn all on the altar, to be a burnt sacrifice, an offering made by fire, of a sweet savor unto the Lord." Or as it is expressed in the Amplified translation "The Lord called Moses out of the tent of meeting, and said to him, say to the Israelites, when any man of you brings an offering to the Lord, you shall bring your offering of [domestic] animals from the herd or from the flock. If his offering is a burnt offering from the herd, he shall offer a male without blemish; he shall offer it at the door of the tent of meeting, that he may be accepted before the Lord. And he shall lay both hands upon the head of the burnt offering [transferring symbolically his guilt to the], and it shall be an acceptable atonement for him. The man shall kill the young bull before the Lord; and the priest, Aaron's son, shall present the blood, and dash it round about upon the altar that is at the door of the tent of meeting. And he shall skin the burnt offering and cut it into pieces. And the sons of Aaron the Priest shall put fire on the altar, and the fat, in order on the wood on the altar; But its entrails and its legs he shall wash with water. And the Priest shall burn the whole on the altar for a burnt offering an offering by fire, a sweet and satisfying order to the Lord." And while time will not permit me to address all of the symbolism contained in these verses there are a few points that I believe must be made if we are going to effectively move forward in our discussion of the Law of Thanksgiving. The first and most important of which is our offerings must be acceptable to God. In these verses as well as the entire first seven chapters of the Book of Leviticus God provided Moses with detailed instructions concerning what was to be offered to Him as well as the purpose for each item to be offered, how it was to be prepared, to whom it was to be presented as well as their response upon presentation. Each of these instructions, were provided to ensure that each offering met Gods exact requirements and specifications, which were necessary for the offering to be accepted by God. It is also important to note that each of the seven sacrifices contained in the first seven Chapters of the Book of Leviticus correspond to a specific aspect of our relationship with God and as a result each was required to be performed in a manner acceptable to God. Second, the offering was required to be personal, each man was required to bring an offering to the Lord as his flock, not the flock of someone else there were no representatives, no proxies and no surrogates. Further each offering was judged individually as oppose to collectively. This become vital because each of us has a personal relationship with Christ and must offer ourselves to Him individually and cannot rely on the worship, Praise or thanksgiving of someone else. Likewise the spirit of God examines each of us to determine the, motivates and the content of our heart. Third what we offer God must be our best. The use of the young bull symbolizes our strength and vitality, our passion, in short the fullness of our gifts. If what we offer to God is going to be acceptable to Him it must not represent what is otherwise useless to us, what is offered as an after thought or what remains after we done or acquired all we desire. God must always be our first priority. Fourth what we offer God must be for God and not ourselves. Any thing that is offered to God for the purpose of drawing attention to us, attempting to persuade God to act or refrain from adding in a certain way or to obtain the approval of anyone other than God will result in the offering being unacceptable to God. This point was made when Jesus taught us that when we performed an act of charity do so in a manner not seeking to be seen because if our motive is to be seen by men we will have no reward from your Father which is in heaven when He declared in the 2nd through 4th verses of the 6th Chapter of the Gospel according to Matthew

" Therefore when thou doest thine alms, do not sound a trumpet before thee, as the hypocrites do in the synagogues and in the streets, that hey may have glory of men. Verily I say unto you, they have their reward. But when thou doest alms, let not thy left hand know what thy right hand doeth: That thine alms may be in secret: and thy Father which seeth in secret himself shall reward thee openly" Or as the Amplified translation states. "Take care not to do your good deeds publically or before men in order to seen by them; otherwise you will have no reward [reserved for and awaiting you] with and from your Father who is in heaven. Thus, whenever you give to the poor, do not blow a trumpet before you, as the hypocrites in the synagogues and in the streets like to do, that they may be recognized and honored and praised by men. Truly, I tell you, they have their reward-in full already. But when you give to charity, do not let your left hand know what your right hand is doing, so that your deeds of charity may be I secret; and you Father who sees in secret with reward you openly." In other words those who are giving offerings in the name of God with the intent of personal gain will find that their offering is not acceptable to God. Lastly and perhaps most important the offering must be done to please God. This point brings us back to our discussions of the first 14 verses of Psalm 50. In the 9th verse of the 50th Psalm God declares "I will take no bullock out of thy house, nor he goats out of thy folds." In other words God was declaring the offerings unacceptable. These offerings were deemed unacceptable by God because they were blemished and the blemish was a result of pride. In this case the pride was found in the motivation for the offering itself a false belief that the reason for providing the offering was because God needed them. If we are truly honest with ourselves we would recognize that many in the body of Christ and perhaps even ourselves see our paying of tithes or giving of offerings more in terms of meeting God's needs as oppose to expressing our thanksgiving to God for the generous way in which He meets ours.

In the 12th verse of the 50th Psalm God declared "If I were hungry, I would not tell thee: For the World is mine, and the fullness thereof." In other words God declared if I was in need, I would not need your help to satisfy it, because I own everything. Therefore when we give to God we should never be so prideful as to think we are supplying His needs but rather should rejoice in the fact that we have an opportunity to thank Him for graciously and faithfully meeting ours. It is this fundamental understanding that God chooses to meet our needs out of His grace not our worthiness upon which thanksgiving is based. But what of our worthiness, some might ask. In today's society especially for those of us fortunately enough to live in western style democracies we have come to believe that we are entitled to live a life of pleasure, prosperity and even privilege by virtue of our birth, but what of our worthiness indeed. Perhaps the better question should be from where did our sense of worthiness or entitlement come? Did it come from God or does it come from our flesh. For that matter upon what is our sense of entitlement based, does it exist by virtue of our birth, our culture, our nation of origin, on of residence, our form of Government, our sense of righteousness, our political, economic, or military power or perhaps we believe that it is intrinsic to our human condition. Once we have come to terms with what we believe to be the source of our perceived entitlement then we can consider a more important question does our perception that any of these factors create a sense of entitlement line up with the perspective God shares with us in His word.

In the 1st and 15th verses of the 28th Chapter of the Book of Deuteronomy the Bible provides that "And it shall come to pass, if thou shalt hearken diligently unto the voice of the Lord thy God, to observe and to do all His commandments which I command thee this day, that the Lord thy God will set thee on high above all nations of the earth: Or as the

Amplified translation states "If you fully obey the Lord God and carefully follow all His commandments I give you today, the Lord your God will set you high above all the nations on earth." And verse 15 states "But it shall come to pass, if thou will not hearken unto the voice of the Lord thy God, to observe to do all His commandments and His statutes which I command thee this day all these curses shall come upon thee, and overtake thee." Or as the amplified translation states "But if you will not obey the voice of the Lord your God, being watchful to do all His commandments and His statues which I command you this day, then all these curses shall come upon you and overtake you." It is clear from both of these verses of scripture that God bases over ability to receive the blessing of God not upon our culture, our social or economic system our nation of origin or residence or the form of government we live under but rather our obedience to His commands. This fact becomes even more evident when we consider that the 28th Chapter of the Book of Deuteronomy, as well as the remainder of the Old Testament, was written to the nation of Israel which were God's chosen people. In fact even a casual review of the Old Testament will reveal that God's promises to bless His people were based on their obedience to His word and not their identity as a people. In addition, it is also evident from Old Testament scripture that the nation of Israel never fully realized the promises God made for their lives because they were unable to meet God's standard for righteousness. This latter point becomes especially important because many believe that the nation of Israel serves as a type and shadow of the New Testament church in which case the Old Testament scripture can, or perhaps should, be seen as painting a picture of the church. Whether or not those who see the Old Testament scriptures as a type and shadow of the New Testament church are correct and irrespective of my personal view on the matter it is clear that every promise we as the New Testament church stand in is derived from the Old Testament covenant made by God on Abraham's behalf. In the 6th through 9th verses of the 3rd Chapter of the Book of Galatians declared "Even as Abraham believed God, and it was accounted to him for righteous. Know ye therefore that they which are of faith, the same are the children of Abraham. And the scripture, foreseeing that God would justify the heathen through faith, preached before the gospel unto Abraham, saying, in thee shall all nations be blessed. So then they which be of faith are blessed with faithful Abraham." Or as the Amplified translation states "Thus Abraham believe and adhered to and trusted in and relied on God, and it was reckoned and placed to his account and accredited as righteousness-as conformity to the divine will in purpose, thought and action. Know and understand that it is [really] the people [who live] by faith who are [the true] sons of Abraham. And the Scripture, foreseeing that God would justify-declare righteous, put in right standing with Himself-the Gentiles in consequence of faith, proclaimed the Gospel [foretelling the glad tidings of a Savior long beforehand] to Abraham in the promise, saying, In you shall all the nations [of the earth] be blessed. So then, those who are people of faith are blessed and made happy and favored by God [as partners in fellowship] with the believing and trusting Abraham." As this scripture unfolds before our eyes it tells the most amazing story that God who knew all things before the beginning, even before the law was given that man, because of his sinful and prideful nature would be unable to obey, sowed the seed of faith through Abraham into all mankind so that righteousness would be afforded to all who would upon hearing the gospel of Jesus Christ choose to believe. That those who choose to believe would no longer be bound by the works of the law but rather live in His grace, not because of what they deserve but because of what they need.

In the 4th through 9th verses of the 2nd Chapter of the Book of Ephesians the Apostle Paul speaking on the subject of our salvation declared "But God, who is rich in mercy, for his great love wherewith he loved us, Even when we were dead in sins, hath quickened us together with Christ, (by grace ye are saved;) And hath raised us up together, and made us sit together in heavenly places in Christ Jesus: That in the ages to come he might show the exceeding riches of his grace in his kindness toward us through Christ Jesus. For by grace are ye saved through faith; and that no of yourselves: it is the gift of God: Not of works, lest any man should boast." Or as the Amplified translation states "But God! So rich is He in His mercy! Because of and in order to satisfy the great and wonderful and intense love with which He loved us, even when we were dead [slain] by [our own] shortcomings and trespasses, He made us alive together in fellowship and in union with Christ. —He gave us the very life of Christ Himself, the same new life with which He quicken Him. [For] it is by grace-by His favor and mercy which you did not deserve-that you are saved (delivered from judgment and made partakers of Christ's salvation). And He raised us up together with Him and made us sit down together-giving us joint seating with Him-in the heavenly sphere [by virtue of our being] in Christ Jesus, the Messiah, the Anointed One. He did this that He might clearly demonstrate through the ages to come the immeasurable (limitless, surpassing) riches of His free grace (His unmerited favor) in kindness and goodness of heart towards in Christ Jesus. For it is by free grace (God's unmerited favor) that you are saved (delivered from judgment and made partakers of Christ's salvation) through [your] faith. And this [salvation] is not of yourselves-of your own doing, it came not through your own striving-but it is the gift of God; Not because of works [not the fulfillment of the Law's demands], lest any man should boast.-It is not the result of what any one can possibly do, so no one can pride himself in it or take glory to himself." In these verses of scripture as well as much of the Apostle Paul's writing He makes it abundantly clear that our salvation, our position of being in right standing with God is not based on our works, our observance of the law or any human effort, it is not our culture, our social or economic systems, our national heritage or systems of government or any other thing that man has made, it is not based on our worthiness but upon His grace, His unmerited favor towards us. In essence God favor towards us fulfilled the requirements of Deuteronomy 28:1 through the life and death of Jesus Christ for all of those who believe and forever removed the sting of the curses of Deuteronomy 28:15 for all those who believed and adhered to and trusted in and relied on God. So then, if we are to receive the blessings of God not based on our works but by His grace upon what is our sense of entitlement based? The short answer is pride and it is this sense of pride that prohibits us from truly offering God our thanksgiving. It stands to reason that if we believe that we are entitled to the blessings that God so, graciously gives, then it also stands to reason that we would fail to recognize the need to offer thanksgiving to God. Our failure to recognize the true nature of our position with God not only results in our operating in a false sense of entitlement but also a failure to have a true appreciation of the generosity God shows towards us as He continually offers us blessings that we do not deserve. This in turns results in our dishonoring God which in effect robs Him of His Glory. In the 27th through 32nd verses of the second Chapter of the 1st Book of Samuel the Bible teaches us the danger of failure to honor God. When it declares "And there came a man of God unto Eli, and said unto him, Thus saith the Lord, Did I plainly appear unto the house of thy father, when they were in Egypt in Pharaoh's house? And did I choose him out of all the tribes of Israel to be my priest, to offer upon mine altar, to burn incense, to wear an ephod before me? And did I give unto the house of thy father all the offerings made by fire of the children of Israel? Wherefore kick ye at my sacrifice and at mine offering, which I have commanded in my habitation; and honourest thy sons above me, to make yourselves fat with the chiefest of all the offerings of Israel my people? Wherefore the Lord God of Israel saith, I said indeed that thy house, and the house of thy father, should walk before me forever: but now the Lord saith, Be it far from me; for them that honour me I will honour, and they that despise me shall not be an old man in thine house. And thou shalt see an enemy in my habitation, in all the wealth which God shall give Israel: and there shall not be an old man in thine house for ever." Or as the Amplified translation states "A man of God came to Eli, and said to him, Thus has the Lord said, I plainly revealed Myself to the house of your father [fore-father Aaron] when they were in Egypt in bondage to Pharaoh's house. Moreover, I selected him out of all the tribes of Israel to be My priest, to offer on My, to burn incense, to wear an ephod before Me. And I gave [from then on] to the house of your father [forefather] all the offerings of the Israelites made by fire. Why then do you kick [trample upon, treat with contempt] My sacrifice and My offering, which I commanded; and honor your sons above Me by fattening yourselves upon the choicest part of every offering of My people Israel? Therefore the Lord the God of Israel says, I did promise that your house and that of your father [forefather Aaron] should go in and out before Me for ever. But now the Lord says, Be it far from Me; for those who honor Me I will honor, and those who despise Me shall be lightly esteemed. Behold, the time is coming when I will cut off your strength and the strength of your own father's house, that there shall not be an old man in your house. And you shall behold the distress of My house, even in all the prosperity which God will give Israel, and there shall not be an old man in your house for ever." In examining this scripture God's response to those who dishonor Him is as evident as it is impactful. As this story unfolds God reminds Eli of the favor and the blessings that God has bestowed upon his family, how He protected them, selected them for a position of honor, how He blessed them, provided them with prosperity not because they earned it or deserved it but because He favored them, because He loved them, because they needed Him. How did they became accustom to the privilege of living under His favor and began to take God's blessings for granted, until the blessing appeared to be an entitlement, something he deserved because of who he is, his family lineage, his sense of self importance. It is amazing how quickly we can become accustom to the favor of God and forget that the blessings we are experiencing are based on God's goodness and not ours, God's mercy and not our worth, how quickly and completely we forget that the blessings we experience are a gift for God and not a payment. It is reasonable for the God who created all things, sustains all things, provides all things to expect that those who, He loves so much that He would sacrifice His own son to redeem from curses they earned and brought upon themselves would recognize the sheer magnitude of the grace He directs towards them and response with thanksgiving. Isn't it reasonable for God to expect that those of us who call upon His name, live in the splendor of His mercy would simply acknowledge the truth. The truth that every good gift comes from Him, that He is the source of all we have and all we hope to achieve. For that matter and perhaps equally important shouldn't the offering of thanksgiving be a natural response to the realization of the countless mercies we experience day by day, the blessings that we receive with such abundance. The offering of thanksgiving should not be something that requires conscious thought but should rise naturally from a soul that acknowledges the goodness of God. Goodness, that is evident throughout God's creation, from the warmth of the sun, the refreshing nature of the rain, to the beauty found in flowers that bloom in the spring, to the brightness of the array of colors in which they can be found, from the most simplistic of all creatures to the complexity of the human soul. Thanksgiving is the key that unlocks the heart of God and begins the journey of exploration into the deepest of who He truly is and who we are not. Thanksgiving is an acknowledgment of our indebtedness to God a debt that can never possibly be repaid. An acknowledgment of His protection it is an acknowledgment of His holiness, His worthiness of all He is. Thanksgiving is the power within each of us to create an atmosphere that will usher us into the presence of God and all of His fullness.

7

THE LAW OF SACRIFICE

The Law of Sacrifice

The Law of Sacrifice states that the more of yourself you are willing to sacrifice for God the more of God's Kingdom you will see

D. L. Wallace

In the 1st and 2nd verses of the 12th Chapter of the Book of Romans, the Apostle Paul wrote " I beseech you therefore brethren, by the mercies of God, that ye present your bodies a living sacrifice, holy, acceptable to God, which is your reasonable service, and be not conformed to this world; but be ye transformed by the renewing of your mind, that ye might prove what is that good, and acceptable, and perfect will of God." Or as the Amplified Translation states "I appeal to you therefore, brethren, and beg of you in view of [all] the mercies of God to make a decisive dedication of your bodies- presenting all of your members and facilities – as a living sacrifice, holy (devoted, consecrated) and well pleasing to God, which is your reasonable (rational, intelligent) service and spiritual worship. Do not be conformed to this world- this age, fashioned after and adapted to its external, superficial customs. But be transformed (changed) by the [entire] renewal of your mind-by its new ideals and its new attitude- so that you may prove [for yourself] what is the good and acceptable and perfect will of God, even the thing which is good and acceptable and perfect [in his sight for you]." The word sacrifice as it is used in this scripture is derived from the Greek word Thusis which itself is derived from the Greek word thuo which means to slaughter and thus having a reference to the act or victim of the sacrifice. Which would translate the Apostle Paul's command to literally mean present your bodies, or as the amplified translation states all your members and facilities, as a living act or victim of sacrifice, holy (devoted, consecrated) and acceptable to God, which is your reasonable service, (it should be noted that the Apostle Paul describes this act of sacrifice as a service or duty and not an option and at least implicitly suggests that our failure to do so is unreasonable in the sight of God). It is also important to point out that this scripture is quite clear that what is required of us is a living sacrifice and not a sacrifice that leads to our literal death. This distinction becomes of great importance when considering the fact that the sacrifice called for in this scripture is literal and not figurative. One of the great errors of some in the modern Church is to presume that many of the commands, instructions and promises of God are figurative or metaphoric rather than literal, an error that in some instances has robbed the body of Christ of much of the power and authority and even the effectiveness God intended. Some might ask, if this command is literal and it is a living sacrifice what does that actually mean or perhaps a better question would be what does God expect? In answering that question let us revisit the definition or the meaning of the word sacrifice as it is used in this scripture. The word for sacrifice as it is used here is Thusia which literally describes either the act or the victim of a sacrifice. So the question we should ask ourselves is should our lives represent the act or the victim of sacrifice, the answer is clearly that our lives should be the act of sacrifice. So then the next question becomes how do we live our lives as an act of sacrifice? I believe that the answer to this question is found in the 2nd verse of the 12th Chapter of the Book of Romans, where the Apostle Paul wrote" And be not conformed to this world but be ye transformed by the renewing of your mind, that ye might prove what is the good, and acceptable, and perfect will of God." Or as it is expressed in the amplified translation "Do not be conformed to this world- this age, fashioned after and adapted to its external, superficial customs. But be transformed (changed) by the [entire] renewal of your mind- by its new ideals and its new attitude- so that you may prove [for yourself] what is the good and acceptable and perfect will of God, even the things which is good and acceptable and perfect [in His sight for you]. "In other words we are commanded to live our lives as a sacrifice of the external, superficial customs of this world by renewing our minds. At this point in our discussion it is important to recognize that it is not simply an admonishment not to sin but rather an exchange of values, customs, ways, expectations, desires, motives, and if I may be so bold, the gods of this world's system in order to discover those of the Kingdom of God. If we were to examine scripture we would discover that the Bible has a great deal to say on this subject and many of the teachings of Jesus address this issue. For example, in the 39th verse of the 10th Chapter of the Gospel according to Matthew. Jesus declared "He that finds his life shall lose it: and He that loseth his life for my sake shall find it" or as the Amplified translation states "Whosoever finds his [lower] life will lose [the higher life], and whosoever loses his [lower] life on my account will find [the higher life]." It should be obvious that the lower life as it is referred to in the amplified translation is the carnal life or the external, superficial life referred to in the 1st verse of the 12th Chapter of the Book of Romans and the higher life is the good, acceptable and perfect will of God. It is even more obvious that it is not possible for us to devote our lives to the pursuit of both, but rather we must choose which life holds greater value to us. In point of fact, Jesus specifically addressed the need to make this choice in the 24th through 33rd verses of the 6th Chapter of the Gospel according to Matthew when He declared" No man can serve two masters: for either he will hate the one, and love the other; or else he will hold to the one and despise the other. Ye cannot serve God and mammon. Therefore, I say unto you, take no thought for your life, what ye shall eat, or what ye shall drink; nor yet your body, what ye shall put on. Is not the life more than meat, and the body than raiment? Behold the fowls of the air: for they sow not neither do they reap, nor gather into barns; yet your heavenly Father feedeth them. Are you not much better than they? Which of you by taking thought can add one cubit unto his stature? And Why take ye thought for raiment? Consider the lilies of the field, how they grow; they toil not, neither do they spin: and yet I say unto you, that even Solomon in all his glory was not arrayed like one of these, wherefore, if God so clothe the grass of the field, which today is, and tomorrow is cast into the oven, shall he not much more clothe you, O ye of little faith? Therefore take no thought, saying, what shall we eat? Or what shall we drink? Or wherewithal shall we be clothed? (for after all these things do the Gentles seek:) For your heavenly Father knoweth that ye have need of all these things. But seek ye first the Kingdom of God, and his righteousness; and all these things will be added unto you." Or as the amplified translation states" No one can serve two masters; for either he will hate the one and love the other, or he will stand by and be devoted to the one and despise and be against the other. You cannot serve God and mammon [that is deceitful riches, money, possessions or what is trusted in]. Therefore, I tell you, stop being perpetually uneasy (anxious and worried) about your life, what you shall eat or what you shall drink, and about your body, what you should put on it. Is not life greater [in quality] than food, and drink, and the body [far above and more excellent] than clothing? Look at the birds of the air; they neither sow nor reap nor gather into barns, and yet your Heavenly Father keeps feeding them. Are you not worth more than they? And which of you by worrying and being anxious can add one unit of measure [cubit] to his stature or to the span of his life? And why should you be anxious about clothes consider the lilies of the fields and learn thoroughly how they grow; they neither toil not spin; yet I tell you, even Solomon in all his magnificence (excellence, dignity and grace) was not arrayed like one of these. But if God so clothes the grass of the field, which today is alive and green and tomorrow is tossed into the furnace, will He not much more surely clothe you, O ye of little faith? Therefore, do not worry and be anxious, saying, what are we going to have to eat? Or, what are we going to have to drink?; or what are we going to wear? For the Gentles (heathen) wish for and crave and diligently seek after these things; and your Heavenly Father well knows that you need them all. But seek for (aim at and strive after) first of all His Kingdom and His righteousness [His way of doing and being right]. And then all these things taken together will be given you besides" what become evident from these scriptures is that we are required to forgo (sacrifice) our desire to live by the values and customs of this world and their emphasis on materialism as a measure of success, self gratification, pride, independence from God, status, vanity, and the goals and priorities of this system and instead pursue Godliness in our hearts and the works of our hands. By way of example lets examine how the world's system views and values success.

Let's say we have Robert, who has not only graduated from an Ivy League college, but has successfully completed a graduate degree in Business. After years of working for a series of fortune 500 corporations Robert launches his own business. Robert's business starts with one employee and grows to a staff of 50. Robert's company manufactures and distributes a line of plastic but life like toys such as assault rifles, army vehicles, and hand grenades. The toys are made in a small village in China rather than a plant in the United States because manufacturing them in China allows Robert to pay the employees .10 cents per hour and Robert does not have to worry about paying for health care or retirement benefits, social security, workmen's compensation or other additional costs his company would have to pay in the United States. In addition, China has little to no regulations relating to the treatment of Robert's employees therefore Robert's company can require it's employees to work long hours with out the burden of having to pay for overtime and is able to fire any employee the company chooses for any reason. In addition, Robert's company sells its toys through a network of independent contractors who because they are not considered employees are not offered any health care insurance, unemployment benefits if their contracts are terminated. Further Robert's company is no required to pay for workmen's compensation insurance for them and contributes nothing to their social security benefits. The independent contractors are paid based solely on commission and are required to use their personal vehicles for their sales calls are not reimbursed for gas or mileage by the company. In addition, the independent contractors are charged back the commission they earn for each item that is returned even if it is returned because it is defective. Robert, who identifies himself as a Christian, had personal income of $28,000,000.00 last year which he managed to keep in off shore accounts to avoid paying income taxes, he lives in a $5,000,000.00 house while his Company's entire payroll, including the commissions paid to the company's independent contractors is less than $1,000,000.00 per year. By the standards of the world Robert's life is a success, but the question is, is Robert's life successful in the sight of God? or to put it in the contact of our discussion is Robert's life an act of sacrifice which demonstrates the good and acceptable and perfect will of God.? I trust that the answer to the question is clear. In fact Robert's life serves to highlight what Jesus taught in the 24th verse of the 6th Chapter of the amplified translation of the Gospel according to Matthew when Jesus said "No man can serve two masters: for he will hate the one, and love the other, or else he will hold to the one and despise the other. Ye cannot serve God and mammon" and it is clear who or what Robert has chosen to serve, but what about us? Are we any different than Robert , we may not have an $5,000,000.00 home and we may not make as much money as Robert does but that is a matter of having the means but does not in and of itself speak to the real issue which is our desire. So then the question really becomes what do we desire, if we are truthful to ourselves do we desire success as the world defines it with wealth, material possessions, status, and the power that it promises or do we desire to live our lives as an act of sacrifice so that we can demonstrate the good, and acceptable, and perfect will of God. For so many in the Body of Christ this is an uncomfortable topic because they believe that it is unfair of God to suggest much less command that they chose between the things of this world and the things of His Kingdom. However what many fail to realize is that their response to this issue simply reveals the choice then have already made. In the 17th through 27th verses of the 10th Chapter of the Gospel according to Mark the Bible speaks directly to this issue in the story of the rich young ruler and provides "And when He was gone forth into the way, there came one running, and kneeled to him, and asked him, Good master, what shall I do that I may inherit eternal life? And Jesus said unto him why callest thou me good? There is none good but one, that is God. Thou knowest the commandments, Do not commit adultery, Do not kill, Do not steal, Do not bear false witness, Defraud not, Honour thy father and mother. And he answered and said unto him, Master, all these have I observed from my youth. Then Jesus beholding him loved him and said unto him, one thing thou lackest: go thy way, sell whatsoever thou hast, and give to the poor, and thou shall have treasure in heaven: and come, take up the cross, and follow me. And he was sad at that saying, and went away grieved: for he had great possessions. And Jesus looked round about, and saith unto His disciples, how hard shall they that have riches to enter into the Kingdom of God. And the disciples were astonished at His words. But Jesus answereth again, and saith unto them, it is easier for a camel to go through the eye of a needle, than for a rich man to enter into the Kingdom of God, and they were astonished out of measure, saying among themselves, who then can be saved? And Jesus looking upon them saith, with men it is impossible, but not with God: For with God all things are possible" or as the amplified translation provides "And as He was setting out on His journey, a man ran up and knelt before Him, and asked Him Teacher, (you are essentially and perfectly morally) good, what must I do to inherit eternal life (that is, to partake of eternal salvation in the Messiah's Kingdom)? And Jesus said to him, why do you call Me (essentially and perfectly morally) good? There is no one (essentially and perfectly morally) good except God alone. You know the commandments: Do not kill; do not commit adultery, do not steal; do not bear false witness; do not defraud; honour your father and mother. And he replied to Him teacher, I have carefully guarded and observed all these and taken care not to violate them from my boyhood. And Jesus looking upon him loved him, and He said to him you lack one thing; go and shall sell all you have and give [the money] to the poor, and you well have treasure in heaven; and come [and] accompany Me- walking the same road that I walk at that saying the man's countenance fell and was gloomy, and he went away grieved and sorrowing, for he was holding great possessions and Jesus looked around and said to His disciples, with what difficulty will those who possess wealth and keep on holding it enter into the Kingdom of God. It is easier for a camel to go through the eye of a needle than [for] a rich man to enter the Kingdom of God. And they were shocked and exceedingly astonished, and said to Him and to one another, then who can be saved. Jesus glanced around at them and said, with men [it is] impossible, but not with God: for all things are possible with God."

In examining this scripture there are a few things that are readily apparent. The first is that the issue that hindered the rich young ruler from getting into the Kingdom was not one of sin. In the 19th and 20th verses of the 10th Chapter of the Gospel according to Mark the Bible addresses the issue of the rich young ruler's sin when it states " Thou knowest the commandments, Do not commit adultery, do not kill, do not steal, do not bear false witness, defraud not, honour thy father and mother and he answered and said unto Him Master, all of these I have observed from my youth." Further, it is evident from Jesus was pleased with his statement. The rich young ruler's issue was not one of his sin but rather one of his willingness to sacrifice. Very often when we think of God's call for our sacrifice we respond with a commitment to offer God a life without sin as if the sins we forgo are themselves an offering to God. However this is untrue. A careful examination of the scripture which provide instructions on the law of sacrifice will make this point clear. In the 1st through 3rd verses of the 1st Chapter of the book of Leviticus the Bible provides" And the Lord called unto Moses, and spake unto him out of the tabernacle of the congregation, saying, speak unto the children of Israel, and say unto them, if any man of you bring an offering of the cattle, even of the herd, and of the flock. If his offering be a burnt sacrifice of the herd, let him offer a male without blemish: he shall offer it of his own voluntary will at the door of the tabernacle of the congregation of the Lord." Or as the amplified translation states" The Lord called to Moses out of the tent of meeting, and said to him, say to the Israelites, when any man of you brings an offering to the Lord, you shall bring your offering from the herd, he shall offer a male without blemish; he shall offer it at the door of the tent of meeting, that he may be accepted before the Lord." There are at least four principles relating to the laws of the offering that preclude the possibility that our agreeing to forgo sin constitutes an offering to God. First, the 2nd verse of the 1st Chapter of the book of Leviticus provides that "if any man of you brings" which suggests that the offering is voluntary. The Bible teaches us that when God gave the Law to Moses the laws were given to Moses as commandments, which the nation of

Israel and in fact all of mankind are required to obey or face punishment.

The second principle is the principle of ownership. The 2nd verse of the 1st Chapter of the Book of Leviticus states If any man of you bring an offering unto the Lord, ye shall bring your offering of the cattle" and thus each man was only allowed to offer an offering that legally belonged to him. In order for the requirement of ownership to be satisfied the person offering the offering must have a legal right to the thing offered and since no man has a legal right to sin, sin could not be offered as any man's offering.

The third principle is the principle of proportionality. Under the principle of proportionality man is required to return a portion of what he has received from God back to God as a mean of sanctifying the remaining portion. Again this principle precludes sin from being an offering to God. First of all man did not derive sin from God or his sinful nature from God and second sin cannot be sanctified by God.

Forth is the principle of acceptability. The 3rd verse of the 1st Chapter of the Book of Leviticus "if his offering be a burnt offering of the herd, let him offer a male without blemish" which means that in order for an offering to be acceptable to God it must be in its original condition without defect and since sin is the greatest of all defects it stands to reason that sin could not be offered to God any more then the blemish that marred the cattle could be. The third and perhaps more important point is that the rich young ruler valued the riches and ways of the world more than he valued entry into the Kingdom. In the 21st verse of the 10th Chapter of the Gospel according to Mark the Bible declares" Then Jesus beholding him loved him and said unto him, one thing thou lackest: go thy way, sell whatsoever thou hast, and give it to the poor, and thou shalt have treasure in heaven: and come, take up the cross, and follow me." The Bible goes on to say that when the rich young ruler heard what Jesus said that "he was sad at that saying, and went away grieved." I think it is quite compelling that the young ruler walked away from an invitation to enter into the Kingdom of God because he was unwilling to pay the price and I am dismayed at the thought of what his choice says about the value, or lack thereof, he placed upon the Kingdom of God, or for that matter what our choices say about the value we place on the invitation to enter the Kingdom of God that Jesus extends to us. Every day of our lives we either choose to live our lives as an act of sacrifice or we choose to be conformed to the image of this world and its external, superficial customs and the choice we make tells God the value we truly place on the Kingdom of God and the value we place on the idols we serve, idols such as security, love, urgency, self-fulfillment, easy, life, fame, approval, success or approval. In the 44th through 46th verses of the 13th Chapter of the Gospel according to Matthew Jesus taught on the subject of the value we should place on the Kingdom when He said" Again, the Kingdom of heaven is like unto a treasure hid in a field; the which when a man hath found, he hideth, and for joy there of goeth and selleth all that he hath, and buyeth that field. Again, the Kingdom of Heaven is like a merchant man, seeking goodly pearls of great price, when he had found one pearl of great price went and sold all he had, and brought it." Or as the amplified translation states" The Kingdom of heaven is like something precious buried in a field, which a man found and hid again; then in his joy he goes and sells all he has and buys that field. Again the Kingdom of heaven is like a man who is a dealer in search of fine pearls, who on finding a single pearl of great price, went and sold all he had and brought it." In these scriptures there are a few issues which need to be examined. First in both of the parables the man engaged in the exchange discovered or found the Kingdom and in so doing had an experience that allowed them or perhaps required them to experience the value of life in Christ or life in the Kingdom. This experience is more than simply going to Church or standing in belief in Christ based on the stories contained in the Bible or the testimony of the presence or power of God in someone else's life. It is a personal experience with God. Far too often in the Body of Christ we have become content with becoming listeners and not seekers and as a result there are far too many who are living in the testimonies of others, without ever really tasting the goodness or experiencing the power of God for themselves. As a result far too many never develop a passion for seeking God in prayer, fasting, worship or even study. Far too many never have an encounter with the King or a glimpse of the Kingdom and see no reason to "sell all" because they do not understand there is more to God that what they possess. The second point is that both men placed great value on the treasure or pearl they discovered than what they were required to exchange for it. In the 1st and 2nd verses of the 12th Chapter of the Book of Romans the Apostle Paul make it clear that the purpose of not being conformed to the image of this world and instead of being transformed by the renewing of our minds is to prove (demonstrate) the good, and acceptable, and perfect will of God. Implicit in this statement is the fact that the good and acceptable and perfect will of God is far better or should I say of far greater value than what is being sacrificed. Let's take a look at this issue of value of the Kingdom in the context of God's promises to the nation of Israel in Deuteronomy 28 and while the promise of the Kingdom is not merely or even primarily physical or economic, I believe the promises contained in Deuteronomy will nonetheless aid our discussion. In the 1st through 14th verses of the 28th Chapter of the Book of Deuteronomy the Bible provides "And it shall come to pass, if thou shalt hearken diligently unto the voice of the Lord thy God, to observe and to do all His commandments which I command thee this day, that the Lord God thy God will set thee on high above all nations of the earth: and all these blessings shall come on thee, and overtake thee, if thou shalt hearken unto the voice of the Lord thy God. Blessed shalt thou be in the city, and blessed shalt thou be in the field. Blessed shall be the first fruit of thy body, and the fruit of thy ground, and the fruit of thy cattle, the increase of thy kine, and the flocks of thy sheep. Blessed shall be thy basket and thy store. Blessed shalt thou be when thou comest in, and blessed shalt thou be when thou goest out. The Lord shall cause thine enemies that rise up against thee to be smitten before thy face: they shall come out against thee one way, and flee before thee seven ways. The Lord shall command the blessings upon thee in thy storehouses, and in all that thou settest thine hand unto; and he shall bless thee in the land which the Lord thy God giveth thee. The Lord shall establish thee an holy people unto himself as he hath sworn unto thee, if thou shalt keep the commandments of the Lord thy God, and walk in his ways. And all people of the earth shall see that thou art called by the name of the Lord; and they shall be afraid of thee. And the Lord shall make thee plenteous in goods, in the fruit of thy body, and in the fruit of thy cattle, and in the fruit of thy ground, in the land which the Lord sware unto thy fathers to give thee. The Lord shall open unto thee his good treasure, the heaven to give the rain unto thy land in his season, and to bless all the works of thine hand: And thou shalt lend unto many nations. And thou shalt not borrow. And the Lord shall make thee the head and not the tail; and thou shalt be above and only, and thou shalt not be beneath; if that thou hearken unto the commandments of the Lord thy God, which I command thee this day, to observe and to do them: And thou shalt not go aside from any of the words which I command thee this day, to the right hand, or to the left, to go after other gods to serve them." Or as the amplified translation provides" If you will listen diligently to the voice of the Lord your God, being watchful to do all His commandments which I command you this day, the Lord your God will set you high above all the nations of the earth. And all these blessings shall come upon you and overtake you if you heed the voice of the Lord your God. Blessed shall you be in the city and blessed shall you be in the field. Blessed shall be the fruit of your body and the fruit of your ground and the fruit of your beast, the increase of your cattle and the young of your flock. Blessed shall be your basket you're your kneading trough. Blessed shall you be when you come in and blessed shall you be when you go out. The Lord shall cause your enemies who rise up against you to be defeated before your face; they shall come out against you one way and flee before you seven ways. The Lord shall command the blessings upon you in your storehouse and in all that you undertake. And He will bless you in the land which the Lord your God gives you. The Lord will establish you as a people holy to Himself, as He has sworn to you, if you keep the commandments of the Lord your God and walk in His ways. And all people of the earth shall see that you are called by the name [and in the presence of] the Lord, and they shall be afraid of you. And the Lord shall make you have surplus of prosperity, through the fruit of your body, of your livestock, and of your ground, in the land which the Lord swore to your fathers to give you. The Lord shall open to you His good treasury, the heavens, to give the rain of your land in its season and to bless all the work of your hands; and you shall lend to many nations, but shall not borrow. And the Lord shall make you the head, and not the tail; and you shall be above only, and you shall not be beneath, if you heed the commandments of the Lord your God which I command you this day and are watchful to do them. And you shall not turn aside from any of the words which I command you this day, to the right hand or to the left, to go after other gods to serve them." Think for a moment if the value of these promises coming to past in your life, how much would that mean to you or more importantly what does the world have to offer you that is worth more. If each of us could only understand the true value of what the Kingdom represents then we would be able to identify with the two men who were the characters in the parables contained in the 44th through 46th verses of the 13th Chapter of the Book of the Gospel according to Matthew. We would also be able to understand the instructions Jesus conveyed to His disciples in the 33rd verse of the 6th Chapter of the Gospel according to Matthew when He said" But seek ye first the Kingdom of God and His righteousness; and all these things will be added unto you." Or as the amplified translation states" But seek for (aim at and strive after) first of all His Kingdom, and His righteousness [His way of doing and being right] and then all these things taken together will be given you besides." It should be clear by now that the command to "seek ye first the Kingdom of God, and His righteousness" is the same command found in the 1st verse of the 12th Chapter of the Book of Romans "Be ye not conformed to this world but be ye transformed by the renewing of your mind" as well as the command in the 1st verse of the 28th Chapter of the Book of Deuteronomy " hearken diligently unto the voice of the Lord thy God, to observe and to do all of His commandments. It should be equally clear that the "all these things shall be added is the same promise as the promise contained in the 1st through 14th verses of the 28th Chapter of the Book of Deuteronomy "the Lord God thy God will set thee on high above all nations of the earth: and all these blessings shall come on thee, and overtake thee, if thou shalt hearken unto the voice of the Lord thy God. Blessed shalt thou be in the city, and blessed shalt thou be in the field. Blessed shall be the first fruit of thy body, and the fruit of thy ground, and the fruit of thy cattle, the increase of thy kine, and the flocks of thy sheep. Blessed shall be thy basket and thy store. Blessed shalt thou be when thou comest in, and blessed shalt thou be when thou goest out. The Lord shall cause thine enemies that rise up against thee to be smitten before thy face: they shall come out against thee one way, and flee before thee seven ways. The Lord shall command the blessings upon thee in thy storehouses, and in all that thou settest thine hand unto; and he shall bless thee in the land which the Lord thy God giveth thee. The Lord shall establish thee a holy people unto himself as he hath sworn unto thee, if thou shalt keep the commandments of the Lord thy God, and walk in his ways. And all people of the earth shall see that thou art called by the name of the Lord; and they shall be afraid of thee. And the Lord shall make thee plenteous in goods, in the fruit of thy body, and in the fruit of thy cattle, and in the fruit of thy ground, in the land which the Lord sware unto thy fathers to give thee. The Lord shall open unto thee his good treasure, the heaven to give the rain unto thy land in his season, and to bless all the works of thine hand: And thou shalt lend unto many nations. And thou shalt not borrow. And the Lord shall make thee the head and not the tail; and thou shalt be above and only, and thou shalt not be beneath; if that thou hearken unto the commandments of the Lord thy God, which I command thee this day, to observe and to do them: And thou shalt not go aside from any of the words which I command thee this day, to the right hand, or to the left, to go after other gods to serve them." Which is the same promises as the demonstration of the good, and acceptable, and perfect will of God referenced in the 1st and 2nd verses of the 12th Chapter of the Book of Romans.

Third both the men in the parables contained in the 44th through 46th verses of the 13th Chapter of the Gospel according to Matthew surrender what they possessed voluntarily. This point cannot be stressed strongly enough!!! In the 1st verse of the 12th Chapter of the Book of Romans the Apostle Paul urges us to "present" our bodies or as it is expressed in the amplified translation "to make a decisive dedication of your bodies-presenting all your members and faculties". In the beginning of the first verse the Apostle Paul says something that I believe gives shape to this entire issue of value, he says I beseech you therefore brethren by the mercies of God or as the amplified translations states it, I appeal to you therefore, brethren, and I beg of you in view of [all] the mercies of God. In other words present your bodies as a living sacrifice not because of what God may do but because of all of what God has already done. This is the essence of any, in fact all, acts of worship, a response to the identity and activity of God. Further both men in the parable contained in the 44th through 46th verses of the 13th Chapter of the Gospel according to Matthew sold their possessions based on what they experienced. In the Body of Christ today there is such an emphasis on what God has promised to do that sometimes we forget the amazing and wondrous things that God has already done and we position ourselves not as worshipers but as negotiators seeking to offer a sacrifice of worship to God based on His willingness to meet our demands while all the while losing sight of the countless blessings that He has already provided, the countless sins He has already forgiven, the countless measure of protection He has already provided, the destiny He has already established all because we are looking at our lives as the world sees and defines them and not the value of the treasure before us. Ultimately and most importantly our willingness to sacrifice is about our desire for God, for God's wisdom, for God's direction, for God's nature.

When I think of the Apostle Paul's appeal to be transformed by the renewing of our minds, I think of a beautiful crystal vase, carefully and skillfully discipled by its maker, the details of its ornate design, the regal nature of its shape, then I imagine the vase has not been stolen by a thief who had no appreciation of its true beauty. I imagine the thief filling the vase with dirt, filth and the most disgusting things, never washing the vase but rather allowing the dirt and filth to cover and encrust the vase until the vase bares little or no resemblance to its original design and is not longer fit for its intended use. Now just imagine the amazing sense of joy the creator experienced after have paid a great price for its return and anticipating it. The creator would no doubt remember the beauty of the vase he once possessed, how perfectly it was designed, its beauty, how uniquely suited it was for its intended use, all the pleasure He would once experience for the vase. Now image the Creator's reaction when he sees the condition of the vase, that the light no longer reflects its brilliance, how the perfection of it design is not longer apparent, how the glory that it once had is now lost. Imagine the sadness and heaviness of heart that the creator experiences witnessing what has become of its beautiful creation, which is no longer fit for its intended use. Now image that God is the creator and we are the vase, the thief was satan and the price paid was Jesus, the dirt and filth are the carnal, sinful and worldly desires that have marred our very nature. Given this scenario we must face a cold and harsh truth simply being saved is not the same as being restored and until we are restored we cannot function as God intended. So then the question becomes how do we become restored? In our story and in our lives the answer is the same we must be washed, washed until every spot, every blemish and every speck of the dirt and filth that has marred the beauty of our creation is washed away. Some of the dirt and filth can simply be washed away by the power or force of the water, (the Holy Spirit) and is easily rinsed away but some spots have been embedded into us and must be cut away. This is where sacrifice comes in, because unlike the vase we to choose what we will hold onto and what we will let go of, through our prayers, our study, our fasting we determine how clean we will become, in short how much transformation will occur. The more willing we are to confront the stronghold and imaginations that have embedded themselves in our minds the more our minds will be renewed, the more we will be filled by the mind and spirit of God, the more we are restored to our original condition. The more we are restored to our original condition the more we are fit for our original function, which is to represent God, our creator, on this earth. But without a willingness to sacrifice the external and superficial customs of this world and the values they establish, it will not be possible because the more of ourselves we are willing to sacrifice for God the more of God's Kingdom we will see.

8
THE LAW OF SEEKING

The Law of Seeking

The Law of seeking provides that whatever you devote your time and energy to is what you will receive or experience.

D.L. Wallace

In the 9th and 10th verses of the 11th Chapter of the Gospel according to Luke Jesus declared" And I say unto you, ask, and it shall be given you; seek, and ye shall find; knock, and it shall be opened unto you. For everyone that asketh, receiveth; and he that seekest findeth; and to him that knocketh it shall be opened." Or as the amplified translation states" So I say to you, ask and keep asking, and it shall be given you; seek and keep on seeking, and you shall find; knock and keep on knocking; and the door shall be opened to you. For every one who ask and keeps on asking receives, and he who seeks and keeps on seeking finds, and to him who knocks and keeps on knocking the door shall be opened." In this scripture Jesus draws a direct correlation between what we seek and what we find or receive. Although many in the Church have espoused the belief that making a consistent request in prayer demonstrates a lack of faith and is different than making a request in prayer and standing in faith waiting for God to perform it. Those who espouse this belief raise the question of what does the Bible mean to seek. I believe that this amounts to a distinction without meaning! Further, it is unclear to me how one can profess to have faith in God and doubt what God promises about seeking and suggest that when we petition God we should simply make our request known to God once and wait on the result, at the risk of stating the obvious, that view is in direct contradiction with the text as it is contained in the amplified. The word seek as it is used in the 9th and 10th verses of the 11th Chapter of the Gospel according to Luke comes from the Greek word "Zeteo" which connotes the active pursuit of the object sought and is itself derived from the Greek word puthanomai which means to ascertain by inquiry further Zeteo is also defined as a search for something hidden and implies the idea of seeking something for which there is an urgent need. In the 5th through 8th verses of the 11th Chapter of the Gospel according to Luke Jesus teaches a parable concerning seeking when the scriptures declares: And he said unto them, which of you shall have a friend, and shall go unto him at midnight, and say unto him, friend, lend me three loaves; for a friend of mine in his journey is come to me, and I have nothing to set before him? And he from within shall answer and say, trouble me not: the door is not shut; and my children are with me in bed; I cannot rise and give thee. I say unto you, though he will not rise and give him, because he is his friend, yet because of his importunity he will rise and give him as many as he needeth" or as the amplified translation states" And He said to them, which of you who has a friend will go to him at midnight and will say to him, friend, lend me three loaves [of bread] for a friend of mine who is on a journey has just come, and I have nothing to put before him; and he from within will answer, Do not disturb me; the door is now closed, and my children are with me in bed; I cannot get up and supply you [with anything]? I tell you, although he will not get up and supply him anything because he is his friend; yet because of his shameless persistence and insistence, he will get up and give him as much as he needs." In other words the energy and passion involved in our seeking will have a direct impact on the outcome of our efforts. In the 6th verse of the 11th Chapter of the Book of Hebrews, the Apostle Paul speaking on the necessity of persistence and insistence in our seeking declared" But without faith it is impossible to please him: For he that cometh to God must believe that he is, and that he is a rewarder of them that diligently seek him." Or as the Amplified translation states" But without faith it is impossible to please God and be satisfactory to him. "For whoever would come near to God must (necessarily) believe that exists and that He is the rewarder of those who earnestly and diligently seek Him (out)." However, despite Apostle Paul's declaration many have become casual in their effort to seek God or His Kingdom. In this scripture Apostle Paul said something that is vital in our understanding of the importance of seeking" For he that cometh to God must know that He is" this is vital because we can never truly seek

God until we first know that He is God. I realize that upon first examination this statement seems simple and some would suggest goes without saying but does it really? Is it evident from the vantage point of our lives, our utilization of our time, energy, resources that we know He is God? When we consider the direction of our lives, the source of our values, our definition of success, the emphasis we place on personal gratification that we know that He is God? Do our responses to those who are sick, alone, exploited, hungry, homeless, abused, unsaved or backslidden suggest that we know that He is God?

As I take a critical look at our lives, goals, values, priorities, and behaviors I am not convinced that we know that He is God. Sure we acknowledge Him as savior or perhaps even Lord but I see little evidence that we know that His is God. Notice I did not question whether we believe that He is a god, but rather whether we know that He is God. For if we truly know that He is God then we must know that there is no other god besides Him. If we know that He is God then we must know that He and not a "big bang" is the creator and sustainer of the heavens and the earth, that He by His power preserves everything in His pre-ordained order. That He and not evolution created man and that man was created in His image and His likeness not that of some prehistoric creature, if we know that He is God then we must know that He is the owner and ruler of all things and that we owe everything including our very lives to Him. Therefore, if we know that He is God what would or should our response to Him be, the obvious answer is, that we should diligently seek Him. In the 2nd through 5th verses of the 20th Chapter of the Book of Exodus, God speaking through His servant Moses declared "I am the Lord thy God, which have brought the out of the land of Egypt, out of the house of bondage. Thou shalt have no other gods before me. Thou shalt not make unto thee any graven image, or any likeness of anything that is in heaven, above, or that is in the earth beneath or that is in the water under the earth: thou shalt not bow down thyself to them, nor serve them: For I the Lord thy God am a jealous God; visiting the iniquity of the fathers upon the children unto the third and fourth generation of them that hate me." Or as the amplified translation states "I am the Lord your God, who has brought you out of the land of Egypt, out of the house of bondage. You shall have no other gods before or besides me. You shall not make yourselves any graven image [to worship it], or any likeness of anything that is in the heavens above, or that is in the earth beneath, or that is in the water under the earth; you shall not bow down yourself to them or serve them; for I the Lord your God am a jealous God, visiting the iniquity of the fathers upon the children to the third and fourth generations of them that hate me" making it clear that He is to be our only God and that we are not to worship any other god. If God is to be our only, what else should we seek other than Him, and if we know that He is our God what else is there to seek? In the world in which we live and even in the Church we seek a variety of things, some seek happiness, some see wealth, other seek status, love, fulfillment, gratification, acceptance, validation, comfort, security, perfection, education, beauty and a host of other things all of which promise a reward for those who seek them but at what point does our pursuit of these things become worship and the things we seek become our gods? At what point does the time and energy we spend seeking these things rob God of worship that rightfully and exclusively belongs to Him? At what point does the importance we place upon these things become the reverence that is due only to God? Some in reading this might be tempted to point to the world we live in and the need to adjust our thinking to give due consideration to the society in which we live and the need for the Church to be relevant, and for those who make such an argument I would ask isn't relevance just another thing we seek or god we raise in His place? I would also remind them of the admonishment issued by the Apostle Paul to the Church at

Rome in the 2nd verse of the 12th Chapter of the Book of Romans when he wrote "And be ye not conformed to this world: but be ye transformed by the renewing of you mind, that ye might prove what is the good, and acceptable, and perfect will of God." Or as the amplified translation states" Do not be conformed to this world-this age, fashioned after and adapted to its external, superficial customs. But be transformed (changed) by the [entire] renewal of your mind- by its new ideals and its new attitude-so that you may prove [for yourselves] what is the good, and acceptable and perfect will of God, even the thing which is good and acceptable and perfect [is His sight for you]." In addition in the 3rd through 8th verses of the 3rd Chapter of the Book of Philippians the Apostle Paul speaking on the importance of not placing greater value on anything than on our seeking Christ stated" For we are the circumcision, which worship God in the spirit, and rejoice in Christ Jesus, and have no confidence in the flesh. Though I might also have confidence in the flesh, if any other man thinkest that he hath whereof he might trust in the flesh I more; circumcised the eight day, of the stock of Israel, of the tribe of Benjamin, an Hebrew of the Hebrews, as touching the law, a Pharisee; concerning zeal, persecuting the Church; touching the law, blameless. But what things were gain to me, those I counted loss for Christ. Yea doubtless, and

I count all things but loss for the excellency of the knowledge of Christ Jesus my Lord: for whom I have suffered the loss of all things, and do count them but dung, that I may win Christ." Or as the amplified translation states" For we [Christians] are the true circumcision, who worship God in spirit and by the spirit of God, and exalt and glory and pride ourselves in Jesus Christ, and put no confidence or dependence [on what we are] in the flesh and on outward privileges and physical advantages and external appearances. Though for myself I have [at least grounds] to rely on the flesh, if any other man considers that he has or seems to have reason to rely on the flesh and his physical and outward advantages, still more have I! Circumcised when I was eight days old, of the race of Israel, of the tribe of Benjamin, a Hebrew [and a son] of Hebrews; as to the observance of the law, I was of [the party of] the Pharisees, as to my zeal I was a persecutor of the Church, and by the law's standards of righteousness-[supposed]. Justice, uprightness and right standing with God- I was proven to be blameless and no fault was found with me. But whatever former things I had that might have been gains to me, I have come to consider as (one combined) loss for Christ's sake. Yes, furthermore I count everything as loss compared to the possession of the priceless privilege- overwhelming preciousness, the surpassing worth and supreme advantage- of knowing Christ Jesus my Lord and progressively becoming more deeply and intimately acquainted with Him, of perceiving and recognizing and understanding Him more fully and clearly. For His sake I have lost everything and consider it all to be have lost everything and consider it all to be mere rubbish (refuge, drugs), in order that I may win (gain) Christ, the anointed one." In these scriptures the Apostle Paul describes a transformation that each of us should not only aspire to but are commanded to undergo, the transformation from one who finds value and as a result seeks the things of this world to one who find value only in God. In these scriptures the Apostle Paul teaches not only what it is to diligently seek God but also demonstrates an example of what our response ought to be if we know that God is God. An example which is further demonstrated in the 10th through 14th when he declared" that I may know him, and the power of his resurrection, and the fellowship of his suffering, being made conformable unto his death; if by any means I might attain unto the resurrection of the dead; Not as though I had already attained, either were already perfect: but I follow after, if that I may apprehend that for which also I am apprehended of Christ Jesus. Brethren, I count not myself to have apprehend: but this one thing I do, forgetting those things which are behind, and reaching forth unto those things that are before, I press towards the mark for the prize of the high calling of God in Christ Jesus." Or as the Amplified translation states" [for my determined purpose is] that I may know Him- that I may progressively become more deeply and intimately acquainted with Him, perceiving and recognizing and understanding [the wonders of His person] more strongly and more clearly. And that I may in that same way come to know the power out flowing from His resurrection [which it exerts over believers]; And that I may so share His sufferings as to be continually transformed [in spirit into His likeness even] to His death, [in the hope] that if possible I may attain to the [spiritual and moral] resurrection [that lifts me] out from among the dead[even while in the body] not that I have now attained [this ideal] or an already made perfect, but I press on to lay hold of (grasp) and made my own, that for which Christ Jesus, the messiah, has laid hold of me and made me His own. I do not consider, brethren, that I have captured and made it my own [yet]; but on things I do-it is my one aspirations: forgetting what lies behind and straining forward to what lies ahead, I press on towards the goal to win the [supreme and heavenly] prize to which God in Christ Jesus is calling us upward." In this discourse the Apostle Paul makes two things clear, the first is that the only thing worth seeking is God, through Jesus Christ. Just imagine what our lives would be like and how much more of the things of God including the mysteries of Christ we would understand if we could manage the value our relationship with Christ as the Apostle Paul did and truly gave the continued development of our walk with Christ the highest priority in our lives instead of allowing our desires for worldly riches, comfort, acceptance and the various idols we raise compete with Jesus for our affections.

The second is that the value of what we are seeking is ultimately determined by the diligence with which we seek the object being sought. Whenever, I think of the Apostle Paul's passionate discussion of his pursuit of Christ Jesus I think of the parable of the Kingdom found in the 44th through 46th verses of the 13th Chapter of the Gospel according to Matthew which read as follows" the Kingdom of heaven is liken unto treasure hid in a field; the which when a man hath bound hidden, he hideth, and for joy thereof goeth and selleth all that he hath, and buyeth that field, again, the Kingdom of heaven is liken unto an merchant man, seeking goodly pearls: who when he had found one pearl of great price, went and sold all that he had and brought it." Or as the amplified translation states" The Kingdom of heaven is like something precious buried in a field, which a man found and hid again; them is his joy he goes and sells all he has and buys that field. Again the Kingdom of heaven is like a man who is a dealer in search of fine and precious pearls; who on finding a single pearl of great price went and sold all he had and brought it." I cannot help but imagine the Apostle Paul finding a pearl of great price that day on the road to Damascus when in the blinding light of God's glory, he heard Jesus call his name for the first time, how he found the revelation of Jesus Christ so valuable, so precious that he turned and gave up everything he placed value on in order to gain more of Jesus, or how the Apostle Peter hearing the pronouncement of Jesus that the Kingdom of God was at hand, walked away from everything he had to follow Jesus. The Bible tells us of the profound impact their decision to seek Jesus and to place seeking Jesus above all else had on their lives and on our. The question is how have we responded to the call of Christ and how will we respond today, will we respond like the Apostles Paul and peter and countless other men and women who made a decision to surrender all to seek Jesus or will we respond like the rich young ruler found the 17th through 27th verses of the 10th Chapter of the Gospel according to Mark who realizing the price which was required to be paid on order to seek Jesus chose to value his earthly position above heavenly glory or perhaps even Judas Iscariot who betrayed our Lord for thirty pieces of silver, selling his heaven estate for earthly riches. The Bible warns us in the 34th verse of the 12th Chapter of the Gospel according to Luke that" For where your treasure is, there will your heart be also". Seeking is above all else a response from our hearts. It is not a matter of ritual, wearing the right clothes, singing the right songs, praying the right prayers, or even membership in the right Church or domination, for while ritual had its place, seeking is first and foremost about having the right priority and that priority is desiring God above all else. Many in the Church today and even some blessed to be in positions of spiritual leadership in the body of Christ have taken the de-facto position that God understands how busy our lives have become and all the things that compete for our time and affection and because God is such a loving and compassionate God and His acceptance our lukewarm devotions to Him. However, the Bible clearly suggests that God has a different point of view. In the 24th through 26th verses of the 16th Chapter of the Gospel according to Matthew the Bible teaches that "Then Jesus said unto his disciples, if any man will come after me, let him deny himself, and take up his cross and follow me. For whosoever will save his life shall lose it: and whosoever will lose his life for my sake will find it. For what is a man profited, if he shall gain the whole world, and lose his own soul? Or what shall a man give in exchange for his soul?" Or as the Amplified translation states "Then Jesus said to His disciples, if any one desires to be my disciple let him deny himself-that is, disregard, lose sight of and forget himself and his own interests-and take up his cross and follow me [cleave steadily to me conform wholly to my example in living and if need be in dying also]. For whosoever is bent on saving his [temporal] life [his comfort and security here], shall lose [external life]; and whosoever loses his life [his comfort and security here] for my sake, shall find [life everlasting] for what will it profit a man if he gains the whole world and forfeits his life – his[blessed] life in the Kingdom of God? Or what would a man give as an exchange for his [blessed] life in the Kingdom of God?" Here again Jesus raises the question of the diligence of our pursuit and the value we place on our relationship with God through Christ compared to the value we place on the social construct of our lives. In this scripture Jesus makes a few points that I believe every believer should understand. The first is that there is a cost associated with discipleship and that price is self denial. Explicit in Jesus' teaching in these scriptures is the fact that we cannot live based on the priorities of this world and be a disciple and that therefore we must chose which life to focus on, the temporal or the eternal. This point is also taught by Jesus in the 24th verse of the 6th

Chapter of the Gospel according to Matthew when Jesus declared "No man can serve two masters: for either he will hate the one and love the other; or else he will hold to the one, and despise the other. You cannot serve God and mammon." Or as the Amplified translations states " No one can serve two masters; for either he will hate the one and love the other, or he will stand by and be devoted to the one and despise and be against the other. You cannot serve God and mammon [that is, deceitful riches, money, possessions or what is trusted in]."

The second is that we must make a conscious decision to Choose Him. In the 24th verse of the 16th chapter of the Amplified translation of the Gospel according the Matthew, the Bible states" Then Jesus said to His disciples, if any one desires to be my disciple, let him deny himself – that is, disregard, lose sight of and forget himself and his own interest- take up his cross and follow me [cleave steadily to me, conform wholly to my example in living and if need be in dying, also]. This choice is not something that automatically occurs when we confess Jesus Christ as our Lord, or when we walk down the isle of a Church to become a member. It occurs when we make the decision to seek Jesus above all else, When I think of the choice to be come a disciple I think about the lesson discipleship Jesus taught in the 57th through

62nd verses of the 9th Chapter of the Gospel according to Luke which states "And it came to pass, that, as they went in the way, a certain man said unto him, Lord, I will follow thee whithersoever thou goest. And Jesus said unto him, Foxes have holes, and birds of the air have nests; but the Son of man hath not where to lay his head. And he said unto another, follow me, but he said suffer me first to go and bury my father. Jesus said unto him, let the dead bury their dead: but go thou and preach the Kingdom of God, and another also said, Lord, I will follow thee, but let me first go and bid them farewell which are at home at my house. And Jesus said unto him, No man, having put his hand to the plough, and looking back, is fit for the Kingdom of God." Or as the Amplified translations states" And it occurred that, as they were going along the road, a man said to him, Lord I will follow you wherever you go. And Jesus told him, Foxes have lurking-holes, and the birds of the air have roots and nests; but the Son of man has no place to lay His head, And He said to another, Become my disciple, side with my party, and accompany me! But he replied, Lord, permit me first to go and bury [await the death of] my father. But Jesus said to him, allow the dead to bury their own dead; but as for you, go and publish abroad though out all regions the Kingdom of God. Another also said, I will follow you Lord, and become your disciple, and side with your party; but let me first say goodbye to those at my home Jesus said to him, no one who puts his hand to the plow and looks back [to the things behind] is fit for the Kingdom of God." As I read this passage of scripture I wonder how many believers respond to the call to seek God respond by telling God they had something more important to do or how many allowed other priorities in their lives to cause them to neglect God and instead choose the things of the world. I shutter to think about the countless opportunities that may have been lost because of a lack of urgency in our response to the call to seek God. How many times have we been called into prayer by God, but missed the opportunity because the time or place was inconvenient? How many times have we felt the urge to read a passage of scripture but the duties and obligations of our lives hindered us? How many times have we missed a church service or a Bible study or a revival because the time conflicted with another commitment or obligation. In short how many times has God called us into a discipleship experience but we told God something else was more important? What does this say about our real commitment to seek God, not the profession we make with our mouths but about the commitment we make with our hearts? What does it really say about what we really value and place our trust in? What about our passion, if we really had a passion and a hunger for God would we respond the way we so often do? More importantly what does our response say to God and what does God or is saying to us about our passion or lack thereof towards Him? More importantly what is His response to us? I believe the answer to this question is found in the 13th through 19th verses of the 3rd Chapter of the Book of Revelations which provides" He that hath an ear, let him hear what the Spirit saith unto the Churches. And unto the Angel of the Church of the Laodiceans write; these things saith the Amen, the faithful and true witness, the beginning of the creation of God; I know thy works, that thou art neither cold nor hot: I would thou wert cold or hot. So then because thou art lukewarm, and neither cold nor hot, I will spew thee out of my mouth; Because thou sayest, I am rich, and increased with goods, and have need nothing; and knowest not that thou art wretched , and miserable, and poor, and blind, and naked: I counsel thee to buy me gold tried in the fire, that thou mayest be rich; and white raiment, that thou mayest be clothes and that the shame of thy nakedness do not appear; And anoint thine eyes with eyesalve, that thou mayest see. As many as I love, I rebuke and chasten: be zealous therefore, and repent" or as the amplified translation" He who can hear, let him listen to and heed what the Spirit says to the assemblies (the Churches) in Laodicea write: There are the words of the Amen, the trusty and faithful and true witness, the origin and Beginning and Author of God's creation. I know you [record of] works and what you are doing; you are neither cold nor hot Would that you were cold or hot, I will spew you out of my mouth! For you say, I am rich, I have prospered and grown wealthy, and I am in need of nothing; and do not realize and understand that you are wretched, pitiable, poor, blind and naked. Therefore, I counsel you to purchase from Me gold refined and tested by fire, that you may be [truly] wealthy, and white clothes to clothe you and to keep the shame of your nudity from being seen, and salve to put on your eyes that you may see those whom I [dearly and tenderly] love, I tell their faults and convict and convince and reprove and chasten- [that is,] I discipline and instruct them. So be enthusiastic and in earnest and burning zeal, and repent- changing your mind and attitude." I wonder how many of us can honestly describe our efforts of seeking God as a burning zeal. At this point it should be evident that God expects us to seek Him with an "earnest and burning zeal" and that the rational, respectable, socially acceptable, balanced, and lukewarm commitment, (if we can honestly call it commitment) is not acceptable to God and will result in our risking being rejected by Him. The Bible warns of this risk of rejection in the 32nd and 33rd verses of the 10th Chapter of the Gospel according to Matthew when Jesus said" whosoever, therefore, shall confess me before men, him will I confess also before My father which is in heaven. But whosoever shall deny me before men, him will I also deny before my father which is in heaven." Or as the Amplified translation states" Therefore, everyone who acknowledges Me before me and confesses me [out of a state of oneness with me], I will also acknowledge before My father who is in heaven, and confess [abiding] in him. But whosoever denies and disowns Me before men, I also will deny and disown before my father who is in heaven." But it is not Jesus' desire to disown us or to spew us out of His mouth, it is His desire to have a tender and loving relationship with us. Likewise God does not command that we seek Him simply for us to acknowledge that He is God and the objective of our worship but rather out of a deeply felt love for us and a desire for what is truly best for us. The Bible teaches us that our relationship with God is truly for our benefit. In the 5th through 8th verses of the 5th proverb King Solomon wrote" Trust in the Lord with all thine heart; and lean not to your own understanding. In all your ways acknowledge Him and He will direct your path. Be not wise in thine own eyes: fear the Lord, and depart from evil. It shall be health to thy navel, and marrow to thy bones." Or as the

Amplified translation provides "Lean on, trust and be confident in the Lord with all your heart and mind, and do not rely on your own insight or understanding, In all your ways know, recognize and acknowledge Him, and He will direct and make straight and plain your paths. Be not wise in your own eyes; reverently fear and worship the Lord, and turn [entirely] away from evil. It shall be health to your nerves and sinews, and marrow and moistening to your bones." In other words it is God's intent that we place our confidence in Him so that He can lead us because His leading us will make our lives to be better than they would be without Him. As I look at the world we live in with all of the temptations, promises of peace, success, happiness, all of the options that are available, I realize just how important it is to seek God. There is so much that may appear true, correct and right that may ultimately harm, trap and enslave us that our only real hope is to constantly seek God. When I think about the damage that has been done to the world in which we live in the name of progress and all the things we are offered I think of the warning the Bible gives us in the 25th verse of the 16th proverb when King Solomon declared "there is a way that seemth right unto a man, but the end thereof are the ways of death" or as the Amplified translation states " There is a way that seems right to a man and appears straight before him but at the end of it are the ways of death". How many times have we made a decision that we were absolutely convinced was the right or perhaps the only thing to do only to watch our good intentions turn into disaster for us or those around us, just think how different those outcomes would have been if we would have sought God first. But one of the things I love about God is His mercy is everlasting and regardless of how big of a mess we get ourselves into He can and will deliver us from it, if we will simply seek Him. For anyone who may be dealing with a situation that is too big for them to fix, or too difficult for them to handle, I want to encourage you to seek God for His solution to your situation because there is no need to try and deal with it on your own when you have God on your side. In the book of Jeremiah the prophet Jeremiah chronicles the time during the Nation of Israel's found themselves in Babylon under Babylonian captivity as a result of their decision to turn away from seeking God and to begin worshiping the god's of its neighbor, (which should serve as a warning to the Church against its current pre-occupation with worldly methods and standards of success) and their attempts to devise methods to free themselves. But in the 11th through 14th verses of the 29th Chapter of the book of Jeremiah, the prophet Jeremiah speaking on behalf of God wrote "For I know the thoughts that I think towards you, saith the lord, thoughts of peace, and not of evil, to give you and expected end. Then shall ye call upon me, and ye shall go and pray unto me, and I will hearken unto you. And you shall seek me, and find me, when ye search for me with all of your heart. And I will be found of you, saith the Lord: And I will turn away your captivity, and will gather you from all the nations, and from all the places whither I have driven you, saith the Lord; and I will bring you again into the place whence I caused you to be carried away captive." or as the Amplified translation states "For I know the thoughts and plans that I have for you, says the Lord, thoughts and plans for your welfare and peace, and not for evil, to give you hope in your final outcome. Then you will call upon me, and I will hear and heed you. Then you will seek me, inquire for and require me [as a vital necessity] and find me when you search for me with all your heart. I will be found by you, says the Lord, and I will release you from captivity and gather you from all the nations and all the places to which I have driven you, says the Lord, and I will bring you again to the place from which I caused you to be carried away captive." I think that this is not only one of the most impactful scriptures in the Bible, but also one of the most compelling cases for seeking God. In this scripture God provides a clear cut and concise plan for our deliverance, restoration and prosperity, seek

Him!!! In addition, through this scripture God reminds the Nation of Israel, by extension all of us, that He has a personal knowledge of His personal plan that He himself has planned for each of us and that it is a good plan, a plan for peace and our welfare not one of evil. Further God invites us to pray and seek Him and promises that we will find Him and with Him our deliverance, restoration and prosperity when we seek Him with all our hearts. I think that it is so amazing that God not once in Jeremiah 29 did God reminded the Nation Israel that they are responsible for their condition, but rather focuses on assuring them of His promise to deliver them. When I think of verse 14, of the 29th Chapter of Jeremiah, I am reminded of the 5th and 6th verses of the 1st Chapter of the Book of James where the Apostle James wrote" If any man lack wisdom, let him ask God, that giveth to all men liberally, and upbraideth not; and it shall be given him, but let him ask in faith, nothing wavering. For he that wavereth is like a wave of the sea driven with the wind and tossed." Or as the Amplified translation provides "If any of you is deficient in wisdom, let him ask of the giving God [who gives] to everyone liberally and ungrudgingly, without reproaching or fault finding, and it will be given him. Only it must be in faith that he asks, with no wavering-no hesitating, no doubting, for the one who wavers (hesitates, doubts) is like the billowing surge out at sea, that is blown hither and thither and tossed by the wind." This is such an amazing promise that God will give us wisdom simply because we ask in faith, no judgment, no fault finding why would any believer choose to live their life based on their wisdom or the wisdom of the world when we have the wisdom of God available. I get excited every time I go before God and ask for His wisdom because I know that God will show me something that I had not thought of, something better than I could have imagined, after all the Bible declares in the 8th and 9th verses of the 55th Chapter of the Book of Isaiah " For my thought are not your thoughts, neither are your ways my ways, saith the Lord. For as the heavens are higher than the earth, so are my ways, and my thoughts than your thoughts." And God grants us access to His thoughts simply by seeking Him. In point of fact, God desires us to learn to think like Him so that we can understand Him and relate to Him, God desires us to see the world, (both the material and the spiritual world) as He sees it. This point becomes even clear as we read the 33rd Chapter of the Book of Jeremiah. In the 3rd verse of the 33rd Chapter of the Book of Jeremiah when God came to the prophet Jeremiah and declared "Call unto me, and I will answer thee, and show thee great and mighty things, which thou knowest not" Or as the Amplified translation states "Call to me and I will answer you and show you great and mighty things, fenced in and hidden, which you do not know- do not distinguish and recognize have knowledge of and understand." God desires to deliver us, restore us, prosper us, reward us as well as grant us wisdom in areas and concerning subject which we do not understand. What is equally evident from scripture, as is the fact that God has a plan for our welfare and not evil and all of this is available if and only if we will seek Him. Because despite God's clear desires towards us whatever we devote our time and energy to is what we will receive or experience.

9
THE LAW OF REST

The Law of Rest

The Law of Rest states that we will never truly accomplish anything until we first enter into His rest.

D.L Wallace

I want to begin this Chapter with a question, how busy are you? Or perhaps the better question is how much time have you or are you making available to rest in God? The answer to this question will in significant part determine whether you will understand much less fulfill the work God has assigned to you or experience what God has planned for your life.

In the 1st verse of the 4th Chapter of the Book of Hebrews the Apostle Paul wrote" Let us therefore fear, lest, a promise being left us of entering into His rest any of you should seem to come short of it" or as the Amplified translation states" Therefore, while, the promise of entering His rest still holds and is offered [today], let us be afraid[to distrust it], lest any of you should think he has come too late and has come short of[reaching] it." In this scripture the Apostle Paul tells us that we should fear coming short of entering into this promise, but why, what is it that the Apostle Paul sees or recognizes about our entering into this rest that is of such importance that the possibility of failing to obtain it should cause fear? In order to understand the importance that Apostle Paul placed on our entering into rest we must understand what He meant by rest. In the 2nd through 4th verses of the 4th Chapter of the Book of Hebrews the Apostle Paul went on to explain "For unto us was the Gospel preached, as well as, unto them: but the word preached did not profit them, not being mixed with faith in them that heard it. For we which have believed do enter into rest, as he said, as I have sworn in my wrath, if they shall enter into my rest: although the works were finished from the foundation of the world. For he spake in a certain place of the seventh day on this wise and God rested the seventh day from all His works" or as the Amplified translation states "For indeed we have had the glad tidings[Gospel of God] proclaimed to us just as truly as they[the Israelites of old did when the good news of deliverance from bondage came to them]; but the message they heard did not benefit then because it was not mixed with faith (with the leaning of the entire personality on God in absolute trust and confidence in His power, wisdom, and goodness) by those who heard it; neither were they united in faith with the ones {Joshua and Caleb} who heard (did believe). For we who have believed (adhered to and trusted in and relied on God) do enter into that rest, in accordance with His declaration that those [who did not believe] should not enter when He said, as I have sworn in my wrath they shall not enter my rest; and this He said although [His] works had been completed and prepared [and waiting for all who would believe] from the foundation of the world. For in a certain place He has said this about the seventh day: And God rested on the seventh day from all His works." In these passages of scripture Apostle Paul describes the "rest" as an experience that is derived from our faith in the Gospel of God, a peace and contentment that has as its basis an adherence to and trust in and reliance on God stemming from the knowledge of the truth of God's promises especially those contained the Gospel. That Gospel being expressed in the language of Jesus testifying about Himself in the 16th and 17th verses of the 3rd Chapter of the Gospel according to John where Jesus said" For God so loved the world, that he gave his only begotten son, that whosoever believed in Him should not perish, but have everlasting life. For God sent not his son into the world to condemn the world; but that the world through Him might be saved" or as it is expressed in the Amplified translation "For God so greatly loved and dearly prized the world that He [even] gave up His only begotten (unique) Son, so that whosoever believes in (trust in, clings to, relies on) His shall not perish (come to destruction, be lost) but have eternal (ever lasting) life. For God did not send the Son, into the world in order to Judge (to reject, to condemn, to pass sentence on) the world, but that the world might find salvation and be made safe and sound through Him" and in the 18th verse of the 4th Chapter of the Gospel according to Luke which declares"

The spirit of the Lord is upon me, because he hath anointed me to preach the gospel to the poor; he hath sent me to heal the brokenhearted to preach deliverance to the captives, and recovery of sight to the blend, to set at liberty them that are bruised" or as the Amplified translation states" The Spirit of the Lord [is] upon me, because He has anointed me[the anointed one, the messiah] to preach the good news {the gospel} to the poor; He has set me to announce release to the captives and recovery of sight to the blind, to send forth as delivered those who are oppressed [who are downtrodden, bruised, crushed, and broken down by calamity]" In other words God so loved the order and system He created that He sent His son to pay the price for man's sin and resulting separation from Him so that He could begin to restore man back to his original position and the only required that man has to meet is his choice to believe. So if a man or woman believes (trust in, clings to, relies on) Jesus why would he or she not rest? When Apostle Paul addressed the promise of entering into His (God's) rest he (the Apostle Paul) paints a picture using the Sabbath first spoken of in the 2nd and 3rd verses of the 2nd Chapter of the Book of Genesis which declares" And on the seventh day God ended His work which he had made; and He rested on the seventh day from all His works which He had made and God blessed the seventh day, and sanctified it: because that in it He had rested from all His works which God had created and made" or as the Amplified translation states" And on the seventh day God ended His works which He had done, and He rested on the seventh day from all His work which He had done and God blessed(spoke good of) the seventh day, set it apart as His own, and hallowed it, because on it God rested from all His work which He had created and done."

In using these verses to paint a picture of the promise spoken of in the 4th chapter of the Book of Hebrews there are a few things that need to be examined. The first is the nature of the Sabbath itself. Most if not all of us understand the Sabbath as it is expressed as a command in the 8th through 11th verses of the 20th Chapter of the Book of Exodus which provides" Remember the Sabbath of the Lord thy God: in it thou shall not do any work, thou, not thy son, not thy daughter, thy manservant, not thy maidservant, not thy cattle, not thy stranger that is within thy gates: For in six day the Lord made heaven and earth, the sea, and all that in them is, and rested the seventh day: wherefore the Lord blessed the Sabbath day, and hallowed it" or as the Amplified translation states" [earnestly] remember the Sabbath day, to keep it holy (withdrawn from common employment and dedicated to God). Six days you shall labor and do all your works, But the seventh day is a Sabbath to the Lord your God; in it you shall not do any work, you, or your maidservant, your domestic animals, or the Sojourner within your gates. For in six days the Lord made the heavens and the earth, the sea, and all that is in them, and rested the seventh day. That is why the Lord blessed the Sabbath day and hallowed it [set it apart for His purpose]" However, many are not aware that the Sabbath day as it is expressed in the 20th Chapter of the Book of exodus is merely a type and shadow of the relationship with God afforded to us by the life and death of Jesus Christ, and it is this greater truth that the Apostle Paul unveils for us to behold in the 4th Chapter of the Book of Hebrews. If we are going to truly understand the full measure of the greater truth concerning the Sabbath rest we must begin at the beginning.

In the first Chapter of the Book of Genesis the Bible describes God's act of creation of the heavens and the earth and culminates in the creation of man on the sixth day. In the 26th through 28th verses of the 1st Chapter of the Book of Genesis the Bible declares "And God said Let us make man in our image, after our likeness: and let them have dominion over the fish of the sea, and over the fowl of the air, and over the cattle, and over all the earth, and over creeping thing that creepeth upon the earth. So God created man in His own image, in the image of God created

He him; male and female created He them. And God blessed them, and God said unto them, Be fruitful, and multiply, and replenish the earth, and subdue it: and have dominion over the fish of the sea, and over the fowl of the air, and over every living thing that moveth upon the earth" or as the Amplified translation states "God said, Let us [father, Son and Holy Spirit] make mankind in our image, after our likeness, and let them have complete authority over the fish in the sea, the birds of the air, the [tame] breasts, and over all the earth and over everything that creeps upon the earth. So God created man in His own image, in the image and likeness of God He created him; male and female He created them. And God blessed them and said to them, Be fruitful, multiply, and fill the earth, and subdue it [using all its vast resources in the service of God and man]; And have dominion over the fish of the sea, the birds of the air, and over every living creatures that moves upon the earth." It is evident that in the beginning man did not have a "work" of his own but rather was called to complete a work designed by and done for God. A work that was to be performed through the wisdom and knowledge of God and by His power, however, the effect of sin and the fall of man was that man began to live and function apart from and in opposition to God. This further resulted in man carrying out activities (works) that became increasingly unrelated to and hostile towards God's order, systems and purposes for creation. As man walked further away from God and God's plan for creation man began to create systems of commerce, development, government, and life devoid of the love, concern, mercy, generosity or redemptive nature of God, a network of systems that serve to exploit God's creation in an attempt to assert their illegitimate source of authority. However, God who is rich in mercy and love, being unwilling to allow His glorious act of creation to be permanently marred, established the Sabbath as a day when man would discontinue the activities which filled and arguably consumed his life in order to re-focus his attention and more importantly his affections on God. The Second thing that must be examined is the curative or redemptive nature of the Sabbath. From the time of man's rebellion man has become increasingly wicked and detached from the God who created him, however man's increasingly sinful nature did not dissuade God from His original intentions towards man and part of God's plan of redemption is found in the establishment of the Sabbath. The point cannot be stated clearly enough that the Sabbath, whether we view it in terms of the type and shadow found in the 20th Chapter of the book of exodus or the fuller picture of its fulfillment found in the 4th Chapter of the book of Hebrews, was established by God as part of God's plan for man's redemption. The Sabbath at its most basic level is a period ordained by God that requires man to shift his attention away from his goals and desires in order to focus his attention on God. This first and foremost requires man to reflect on the fact that God exists and is the actual creature and owner of all creation and secondly reminds man of his dependence upon God for everything.

In its larger context the Sabbath serves as an invitation from God for man to re-establish the fellowship loss as a result of man's sin and in that regard is the beginning of God's efforts of redemption and restoration this is true because the essence of the Sabbath is the rest from all the activities which are done for man's glory in order to allow man the opportunity to hear from and respond to God. In addition, it is this redirection of man's activities towards God for God's glory that made the Sabbath hallowed.

The third and final point of examination in our discussion of the Sabbath is that the Sabbath is Holy. In the 8th verse of the 20th Chapter of the Book of Exodus instructs us to Remember the Sabbath day to keep it holy therefore it is not enough simply for us to rest from our labor and substitute our work for leisure or dedicate a few hours to attend a service in God's name as many do today. In order to honor the Sabbath and keep it holy we must deliberately focus our attention on God. If we look at the commandment to remember the Sabbath to keep it holy in the context of a substitution of those activities that have as their sole purpose the glorification and fulfillment of man for those which honor and glorify God, even if man derives some benefit, then we can better understand the power and importance of the Sabbath, (whether it is view from the prospective of the 20th Chapter of the book of Exodus or the 4th Chapter of the Book of Hebrews). However, in the 4th Chapter of the Book of Hebrew the Apostle Paul speaks of the Sabbath rest in a manner that is quite distinctive from the commandment to keep the Sabbath day as expressed by Moses in the 20th Chapter of the Book of Exodus. In the 4th Chapter of the Book of Hebrews the Apostle Paul speaks of the Sabbath rest, not as an command or obligation but rather as a promise, something not merely to be observed, but something to be desired, something that results in great benefit to those who obtain it and corresponding great loss to those who do not. It is very telling that the Apostle Paul, who was himself a Jewish scholar and therefore fully aware of the commands and traditions practiced by the Jews would argue that those who observed the Sabbath day contained in the 20th Chapter of the Book of Exodus had failed to enter into the

Sabbath rest because of their unbelief in the Gospel of God and would further describe the rest referenced in this scripture as one which could only have been given to them by Jesus. At the core of the distinction made by the Apostle Paul is an understanding that the Sabbath day served as an example of something greater to come that only those who placed their faith in God would be able to receive. In the 2nd verse of the 4th Chapter of the Amplified translation of the book of Book of Hebrews, the Apostle Paul wrote" For indeed we have had the glad tidings [gospel of God] proclaimed to us just as truly as they [the Israelites of old did when the good news of deliverance from bondage came to them]; but the message they heard did not benefit them, because it was not mixed with faith (with the leaning of the entire personality on God in absolute trust and confidence in His power, wisdom and goodness) by those who head it; neither were they united in faith with the ones [Joshua and Caleb] who heard (did believe). In this Scripture, the Apostle Paul makes reference to God's promises to Abram in the 1st through 3rd verses of the 12th Chapter of the Book of Genesis, which provide "Now the Lord had said unto Abram, get thee out of thy country, and from thy kindred, and from thy father's house unto a land that I will show thee: and I will make of thee a great nation, and I will bless thee, and make thy name great; and thou shalt be a blessing: and I will bless them that bless thee, and curse him that curseth thee: and in thee shall all the families of the earth be blessed" or as the Amplified translation states " Now [in Haran] the Lord said to Abram, go for yourself [for your own advantage] away from your country, from your relatives and your father's house to the land that I will show you. And I will make of you a great nation, and I will bless you [with abundant increase of favors] and make your name famous and distinguished and you will be a blessing [dispensing goods to others]. And I will bless those who bless you [who confer prosperity or happiness upon you] and curse him who curses or uses insolent language towards you; in you will all the families and kindred of the earth be blessed [and by you they will bless themselves]". In order to truly understand the importance of the Sabbath rest discussed by the Apostle Paul it is necessary to take a careful look at the text of the scripture. In this scripture God gives Abram a command followed by seven distinct promises, God commanded Abram to "get thee out" and then promised Abram that He would 1) show him a promised land; 2) make of him a great nation; 3) Bless him; 4) make his name great; 5) that he shall be a blessing; 6) that God will bless them that bless him and curse them that curse him; 7) that from him all the nations of the earth would be blessed. Which establishes the relationship between God and man upon which the promise of the Sabbath rest is based, God works and man follows. Note that the singular instruction that God gave Abram was for him to leave where he was and what he was doing (his work) and follow God. In response God would establish Abram in God's promises for him. However, in order for Abram to fulfill this singular requirement placed upon, Abram would have to have faith in God, because without faith Abram would never cease from his own works and follow God. When the Bible speaks of faith in or belief in God it speaks of more than mere mental acknowledgment of God's existence or attributes it speaks to trust in and reliance upon God that will allow us to enter into the Sabbath rest promised by God.

In the 2nd verse of the 4th Chapter of the Amplified translation of the Book of Hebrews the Apostle draws a distinction between Joshua and Caleb and the rest of the Nation of Israel who failed to believe God based on God's treatment of them in the 13th and 14th Chapters of the Book of Numbers. The 13th Chapter of the Book of Numbers contains the account of the Lord commanding Moses to send the twelve spies into the land of Canaan to observe the Canaanites and bring a report back to Moses. In 25th through 33rd verses of the 13th Chapter of the Book of Numbers speaking concerning the twelve spies provides "And they returned from searching of the land after forty days. And they went and came to Moses and Aaron, and to all the congregation of the Children of Israel, unto the wilderness of Paran, to Kadesh; and brought back word unto them, and unto all the congregation, and showed them the fruit of the land. And they told him and said, we came unto the land wither thou sentest us; and surely it floweth with milk and honey; and this is the fruit of it. Nevertheless the people be strong that dwell in the land, and the cities are walled, and very great: And moreover we saw the children of Anak there. The Amalekites dwell in the land of the south: and the Hitites, and the Jebusites, and the Amorites, dwell in the mountains: and the Canaanites dwell by the sea, and by the coast of Jordan. And Caleb stilled the people before Moses, and said, Let us go up at once, and possess it: For we are well able to overcome it. But the men that went up with him said we be not able to go up against the people; for they are stronger than we. And they brought up an evil report of the land which they had searched unto the Children of Israel, saying, the land, through which we have gone to search it, is a land that eateth up the inhabitants thereof; and all the people that we saw in it are men of a great stature and there we saw the giants, the sons of Anak, which come of the giants: and we were in our own sight as grasshoppers, and so we were in their sight. Or as the Amplified translation states "And they returned from scouting out the land after forty days. They came to Moses and Aaron and to the entire Israelites congregation in the wilderness of Paran at Kadesh, and brought them word, and showed them the land's fruit. They told Moses, We came to the land to which you sent us; surely it flows with milk and honey. This is its fruit. But the people who dwell there are strong, and the cities are fortified and very large; moreover, there we saw the sons of Anak [of great stature and courage]. Analek dwells in the land of the south (the negeb); the Hitites, the Jebusite, and the Amorites dwell in the hill country; and the Canaanites dwell by the sea along the by the side of the Jordan [river]. Caleb quieted the people before Moses, and said let us go up at once and possess it; we are well able to conquer it. But his fellow scouts said, we are not able to go up against the people [of Canaan], for they are stronger than we are. So they brought the Israelites an evil report of the land which they had scouted out saying the land through which we went to spy it out is a land that devours its inhabitants. And all the people that we saw in it are men of great stature. There we saw the nephilim [or giants], the sons of Anak, who come from the giants. And we were in our own sight as grasshoppers, and so we were in their sight" It is evident from the scripture that the twelve spies, (with the exception of Joshua and Caleb) did not have faith in God. The testimony of the spies was quite interesting, in their testimony they acknowledged that the land was good, flowed with milk and honey just as God has promised. However, instead of taking the condition of the land as an assurance that God is a God who fulfills His promises or even recounting the stories of how God defeated Pharoah, parted the red sea, provided water from a rock, provided them manna in the morning and mama in the evening, they dismissed all of the evidence of God's faithfulness and God's power and rejected God's promise because they chose to trust in what they saw over what God said. They as we often do, choose to reject God's true nature and instead subject God to limitations based on what their natural senses determine to be possible or plausible. In short they chose to trust what they saw above what God said which is particularly troubling in light of what the Bible says about faith. In the 1st and 6th verses of the 11th Chapter of the Book of Hebrews the Bible declares "Now faith is the substance of things hoped for the evidence of things not seen….. But without faith it is impossible to please him: for He that cometh to God must believe that He is, and that He is a rewarder of them that diligently seek Him" or as the Amplified translation states" Now faith is the assurance (the confirmation, the title deed) of the things [we] hope for, being the proof of things [we] do not see and the conviction of their reality [faith perceiving as real fact what is not revealed to the senses] …. But without faith it is impossible to please and be satisfactory to Him. For whoever would come near to God must[necessarily] believe that God exists and that He is the rewarder of those who earnestly and diligently seek Him [out]."

If faith is as the Apostle Paul describes it the evidence of things hoped for, the substance of which is unseen, then the Nation of Israel was truly without faith and if without faith it was impossible to please God. Further, given their unwillingness to trust God to fulfill the very promise that not only shaped their identity but also defined their destiny how could they ever please God, for that matter how can we? How can those of us who base our relationship with God upon our belief that we have received salvation, deliverance, restoration or redemption through our faith in Jesus Christ hope to please God if we are not willing to trust Him and rely upon Him enough to allow Him to direct our lives or shape our identities and our destinies. The short answer is we cannot, no work, no good deeds no act of sacrifice or worship will ever have any hope of pleasing God when it is performed by a hand controlled by a heart that lacks faith, because it is our faith and only our faith that justifies us in the eyes of God. I believe at this point the words of the Apostle Paul in the 1st through 3rd verses of the 4th Chapter Book of Hebrews bare repeating

"let us therefore fear, lest a promise being left us of entering into His rest, any of you should seem to come short of it. For unto us was the gospel preached, as well as unto them: But the word preached did not profit them, not being mixed with faith in them that heard it. For we which have believed do enter into rest, as he said, as I have sworn in my wrath, if they shall enter into my rest: although the works were finished from the foundation of the world" or as the Amplified translation states" Therefore, while the promise of entering His rest still holds and is offered [today], let us be afraid [to distrust it] lest any of you should think he has come too late and has come short of [reaching] it. For indeed we have had the glad tidings [Gospel of God] proclaimed to us just as truly as they [the Israelites of old did when the good news of deliverance from bondage came to them]; but the message they heard did not benefit them, because it was not mixed with faith (with the leaning of the entire personality on God in absolute trust and confidence in His power; wisdom, and goodness) by those who heard it; neither were they united in faith with the ones [Joshua and Caleb] who heard (did believe). For we who have believed (adhered to and trusted in and relied on God) do enter that rest, in accordance with His declarations that those [who did not believe] should not enter my rest; and this He said although [His] works had been completed and prepared [and waiting for all who would believe] from the foundation of the world."

In order to truly understand the importance the Apostle Paul places on entering into the Sabbath rest there are two key points which need to be addressed. The first is without faith it is impossible to obtain the promise of rest. In the 3rd verse of the 4th Chapter of the Book of Hebrews, (Amplified) the Apostle Paul wrote " For we who have believed (adhered to and trusted in and relied on God) do enter that rest, in accordance with His declaration that those {who did not believe} should not enter when He said, as I swore in my wrath, they shall not enter into my rest; and this He said although [His] works had been completed and prepared[and waiting for all who would believe] from the foundation of the world" which means that God has sworn that no one who lacks faith shall receive the promise that God has prepared for them. In the 1st through 33rd verses of the 14th Chapter of the Book of Numbers sets forth the events surrounding the nation of Israel's response to the report of the twelve spies. And God's response to their lack of faith and provides "and all the congregation lifted up their voices, and cried; and the people wept that night. And all the children of Israel murmured against Moses and against Aaron: and the whole congregation said unto them, would God that we had died in the land of Egypt! Or would that we had died in the wilderness! And wherefore hath the Lord brought us unto this land, to fall by sword, that our wives and our children should be a prey? Were it not better for us to return into Egypt? And they said one to another, Let us make a captain, and let us return Egypt. Then Moses and Aaron fell on their faces before all the assembly of the congregation of the children of Israel. And Joshua the son of Nun, and Caleb the son of Jephunneh, which were of them that searched the land, rent their clothes. And they spake unto all the company of the children of Israel, saying, the land which we passed through to search it is an exceeding good land. If the Lord delights in us, then He will bring us into this land, and give it us; a land which floweth with milk and honey. Only rebel not ye against the Lord, neither fear ye the people of the land; for they are bread for us: their defence is departed from them, and the Lord is with us: Fear them not. But all the congregation bade stone them with stones. And the glory of the Lord appeared in the tabernacle of the congregation before the children of

Israel. And the Lord said unto Moses how long will this people provoke me? And how long will it be ere they believe me, for all the signs which I have shown among them? I will smite them with the pestilence, and disinherit them, and will make of thee a greater nation and mightier than they and Moses said unto the Lord, then the Egyptians shall hear it (for thou broughtest up these people in thy might from among them:) and they will tell it to the inhabitants of this land: For they have heard that thou Lord art among this people, that thou Lord art seen face to face, and that thy cloud standeth over them, and that thou goest before them, by day time in a pillar of a cloud, and in a pillar of fire by night, now if thou shalt kill all this people as one man, then the nations will have heard the fame of thee will speak saying because the Lord was not able to bring this people into the land which He sware unto them, therefore He hath slain them in the wilderness. And now, I beseech thee, let the power of my Lord be great, according as thou hast spoken saying The Lord is longsuffering, and of great mercy, forgiving the iniquity and transgression, and by no means cleaning the guilty, visiting the iniquity of the fathers upon the children unto the third and fourth generations. Pardon, I beseech thee, the iniquity of this people according unto the greatness of thy mercy, and as thou hast forgiven this people, from Egypt even until now.

And the Lord said, I have pardoned according to thy word: But as truly as I live, all the earth shall be filled with the glory of the Lord. Because all those men which have seen my glory, and my miracles, which I did in Egypt and in the wilderness, and have tempted me now these ten times, and have not hearkened to my voice; surely they shall not see the land which I sware unto their fathers neither shall any of them that provoked me see it: But my servant Caleb, because he had another spirit within him, and hath followed me fully, him will I bring into the land where into he went; and his seed shall possess it. (now the Amalikites and the Canaanites dwelt in the valley) Tomorrow turn you, and get you into the wilderness by the way of the red sea. And the Lord spake unto Moses and Aaron, saying How long shall I bear with this evil congregation, which murmurings of the children of Israel, which they murmured against me. Say unto them, as truly as I live, saith the Lord, as ye have spoken in mine ears, so will I do to you: Your carcasses shall fall in this wilderness; and all that were numbered of you, according to your whole number, from twenty years old and up ward, which have murmured against me. Doubtless ye shall not come into the land, concerning which I sware to make you dwell therein save Caleb the son of Jephunneh, and Joshua the son of Nun. But your little ones, which ye said should be prey, them will I bring in, and they shall know the land which ye have despised. But as for you, your carcasses, they shall fall in this wilderness and your children shall wander in the wilderness forty years, and bear your whoredoms, until your carcasses be wasted in the wilderness" or as the Amplified translation states " And all the congregation cried out with a loud voice, and [they] wept that night: All the Israelites grumbled and deplored their situation, accusing Moses and Aaron to whom the whole congregation said, would that we had died in Egypt: or that we had died in this wilderness: Why does the Lord bring us to this land to fall by the sword? Our wives and little ones will be prey. Is it not better for us to return to Egypt? And they said one to another. Let is choose a captain and return to Egypt. Then Moses and Aaron fell on their faces before all the assembly of Israelites. And Joshua son of Nun and Caleb son of Jephunneh, who were among the scouts who had searched the land, rent their clothes and they said to all the company of Israelites, the Land through which we passed as scouts in an exceedingly good land. If the Lord delights in us, then He will bring us into this land and give it to us, a land flowing with milk and honey. Their defense is departed only do not rebel against the Lord, neither fear the people of the land, for they are bread for us. Their defense and the shadow [of protection] is removed from over them, but the Lord is with us. Fear them not. But all the congregation said to stone [Joshua and Caleb] with stones. But the glory of the Lord appeared at the tent of meeting before all the Israelites. And the Lord said to Moses, how long will this people provokes (spurn, despise) Me? And how long will it be before they believe me [trusting in, relying on, cling to me], for all the signs which I have performed among them? I will smite them with pestilence and disinherit them, and will make of you a greater nation and mightier that they. But Moses said unto the Lord, then the Egyptians shall hear it for you brought up this people in thy might from among them; and they will tell it to the inhabitants of this land. They have heard that you, Lord, are in the midst of this people [of Israel], that you, Lord, are seen face to face, and that your cloud stands over them, and that you go before them in a pillar of cloud by day and in a pillar of fire by night. Now if you kill all this people as one man, then the nations that have heard your fame will say, because the Lord was not able to bring this people into the land which He swore to give to them, therefore He has slain them in the wilderness. And now, I pray you, let the power of my Lord be great, as you have promised, saying the Lord is long-suffering and slow to anger, and abundant in mercy and loving-kindness, forgiving iniquity and transgressions; but He will by no means clear the guilty, visiting the iniquity of the fathers upon the children upon the third and fourth generations. Pardon I pray you, the iniquity of this people according to the greatness of your mercy and loving-kindness, just as you have forgiven [them] from Egypt until now. And the Lord said, I have pardoned according to your word. But truly as I live and as all the earth shall be filled with the glory of the Lord, because all those men who have seen my glory and my [miracles] signs which I performed in Egypt and in the wilderness, yet have tested and provoked me these ten times and have not heeded my voice, surely they shall not see the Land which I swore to give their fathers; not shall any who provoked (spurned, despised) me see it. But my servant Caleb, because he has a different spirit and has followed me fully, I will bring into the land into which he went, and his descendants shall possess it. Now because the Amalekites and the Canaanites dwell in the valley, tomorrow turn and go into the wilderness by way of the red sea. And the Lord said to Moses and Aaron, How long will this evil congregation murmur against me? I have heard the complaints the Israelites Murmur against me. Tell them, as I live, say the Lord, what you have said in my hearing I will do to you: Your dead bodies shall fall in this wilderness-of all who were numbered of you, from twenty years old and upward, who have murmured against me, surely none shall come into the land in which I swore to make you dwell, except Caleb son of Jephunneh and Joshua son of Nun. But your little ones whom you said would be prey, them will I bring in and they shall know the land which you have despised and rejected. But as for you, Your dead bodies shall fall in this wilderness. And your children shall be wanderers and Shepherd in the wilderness for forty years and shall suffer for your whoredoms (your infidelity to your espoused God), until your corpses are consumed in the wilderness." In this scripture God makes three things abundantly clear, the first is that the nation of Israel much like the Church has ample evidence of His power and His intentions towards His people to warrant their trust and reliance upon Him as oppose to what they see. I find it quite amazing how many of us recount the numerous times that God has blessed us, protected us, delivered us, and even warned us, while at the same time refusing to surrender our will or our works so that we can truly walk in obedience and submission to Him. What is even more amazing is how often we ask God to intervene in a given situation while at the same time resist Him because the manner in which He chooses to intervene is not what we would have chosen. Never realizing that not only does God know the plan that He has purposed for each of us but also that that plan and every action requires to be performed by God for its completion was completed before the foundation of the worlds.

The second is that unless we enter into God's promises we will spend our lives wandering in the wilderness only to live our lives and even die with an unfilled promise. Or even worse, through our lack of faith, sentence our children to the same fate. As I contemplate this unsettling truth I think about how many in the Church much less the world are living their lives based on their own plan and based on their own power, how many have no knowledge of God's true plan for their lives and have never experience God's power working to perform what He declared as His will. Perhaps what is even worse is that many who live with out knowledge of God's plan for their lives teach their children (either by word or by example) that they are free or for that matter obligated to determine what they should accomplish with their lives and must rely on their own personal will, determination, and ability to cause it to come to pass. Whenever, I think about people who live based on their own plan and based on their own power, I think about the words of Jesus found in the 31st through 33rd verses of the 6th Chapter of the Gospel according to Matthew which provides " Therefore, take no thought, saying, what shall we eat? Or what shall we drink? Or wherewithal shall we be clothes? (for after all these things do the gentiles seek:) For your heavenly father knoweth that ye have need of all these things: But seek ye first the Kingdom of God, and His righteousness; and all these things shall be added to you. When I read this scripture I hear an invitation to enter into the rest of God, a place where God directs and provides and we obey and respond. However, In order to enter into the rest of God we must believe.

The third is how God responds to our lack of faith. Throughout the Bible we are taught the importance of our faith from the Apostle Paul's declarations in the 6th Chapter of the Book of Hebrews, that without faith it is impossible to please God, to Jesus' declaration to the 9th Chapter of the Gospel according to Matthew that it will be done to us according to our faith, but I believe that the clearest and most dramatic discussion concerning faith is found in the 14th Chapter of the Book of Numbers. Not only does the Lord tell the Nation of Israel that they will not receive the promise He made to their fathers, but God disinherits them which means the promise is no longer theirs and there is no chance of their redemption. Further, their persistent lack of faith has resulted in their being disqualified from the blessing that has defined them and sentenced them to a life of poverty and purposefulness as they are forced to live only long enough to see their replacements receive the promise of purpose and property that was once theirs. However the most troubling part of this revelation is not what happened to the Nation of Israel, but what is happening to the Church The truth of the matter is that many in the Church are suffering the same fate, there are so many who have confessed Christ but still do not know or believe God's promises towards them and as a result do not submit to His will for their lives. So many who even after they have acknowledged Jesus Christ as their Lord continue to pursue the same goals, plans and ambitions as the did before they came to Christ, still live a life based on the wisdom of the world as they strive to live a life of their creation based on their own power, the "self made" men and women who have limited the impact of having Jesus Christ in their life to solving problems and going to heaven when they die never knowing what it means to rest in God. To enter into the rest of God is to recognize and believe that the words of the Prophet Jeremiah spoke in the 11th through 14th verses of the 29th Chapter of the Book of Jeremiah which provide " For I know the thoughts that I think towards you, saith the Lord, thoughts of peace, and not of evil, to give you an expected end. Then shall ye call upon me, and ye shall go and pray unto me, and I will hearken unto you. And ye shall seek me, and find me, when ye shall search for me with all your heart. And I will be found of you, saith the Lord: And I will gather you from all the nations and from all the places whither I have driven you, saith the Lord; And I will bring you again into the places whence I caused you to be carried away captive" or as the Amplified translation states " For I know the thoughts and plans that I have for you, says the Lord, thoughts and plans for welfare and peace, and not for evil, to give you hope in your final outcome. Then you will call upon Me, and you will come and pray to Me, and I will hear and heed you. Then you will seek Me, inquire for and require me [as a vital necessity] and find Me when you search for Me with all of your heart" were spoken specifically to you by God Himself and that they express His clear intentions towards you and to trust that despite your problems, your past or your current circumstances God has the power to bring His intentions towards you to past. To trust God enough to learn His ways and follow His directions instead of being subject to the whims of the world or your own will. To recognize that God and not you are responsible for your life. It is the peace that comes from trusting in the provision and protection of God. The simple truth is that our thoughts, despite how well intended or carefully developed are not His thoughts and our ways are not His ways nor will they bring about His will and it is His will and not ours that we are called to fulfill. The only way we can do that is to enter into His Sabbath rest because we will never truly accomplish anything until we enter into His rest.

CONCLUSION

In Conclusion, as we endeavor to draw closer to God and to live more completely in His divine will, it is helpful if we take our clues from God Himself. Over the more than two thousand years of Christian history we have seen more that a few examples of the dangers of taking our clues from what we concluded within ourselves to be right only to later discover how flawed our conclusions were and the damage that the actions taken as a result of our conclusions has cause.

The most tragic part of it all is the realization that none of the damaged caused was necessary. From the fall of Man in the book of Genesis to the prophetic picture of the things to come given to John on the isle Patmos God has been providing us with detailed instructions on how to live the life that He has ordained for us and we so desperately need. Not only has God provided us these instructions throughout scripture but throughout the generations has sent us prophets, and inspired teachers as reminders of the need to turn our attention and affections towards Him and to place our trust in His ways. This work is yet another one. It is the goal of this work to invite the reader to take a closer look at the foundational issues of their life to determine whether or not they are built on the instructions given to us by God and whether or not they create opportunities for the power of God to be released in our lives. Regardless of our denominational backgrounds or doctrinal belief I believe that each of us hold firm to the belief that God is a loving God and desires the very best for us. I believe that it is also generally understood that our ability to understand God's instructions for our lives and our willingness to obey them are keys to our positioning ourselves to receive more of God's love and His blessings. It is my hope that this work helps in that regard. The eight laws that are discussed in this book are laws which are essential to developing the type of life that is pleasing God and opens the door for the release of God power in the lives of those who learn to operate them. It was my intention to address each of these laws in a very practical way so that the reader can not only understand the importance of each law but understand how they effect their lives and to give them the tools that address those areas of their lives where the laws need to be applied. I pray that I have succeeded…

AUTHOR

Dr. D. L. Wallace was born in Pittsburgh, Pa. Where he graduate from The University of Pittsburgh with a Bachelors Degree in Political Science and History. After obtaining His bachelors Degrees Dr. Wallace went on to obtain a Juris Doctorate from the University of Pittsburgh School of law in 1988 and a Masters at Letters at Law in Taxation and Commerce from the Dickenson college of law in 1991 and has subsequent been awarded a Doctorate in Divinity and a Doctorate in Philosophy. Dr. Wallace accepted Jesus Christ as his Lord and Savior at the age of Nineteen and hear the Lord call him into service at age twenty six. Since that time Apostle Wallace as devoted his life to becoming a dedicated servant of the Lord in 1991 Dr. Wallace move to Atlanta Georgia and has served in numerous roles in a number of ministries in the Atlanta area. Dr. Wallace has been used by the Lord to establish various leadership structures, prison and outreach ministries, and Churches. In 1997 the Lord called Dr. Wallace to serve as the Founder and presiding prelate of Greater Deliverance Global Ministries an Atlanta based ministry founded to build and strengthen ministries and build effective leaders who will bring God's order and presence back to Churches and Ministries in the United States and abroad. Under Greater Deliverance Global Ministries Dr. Wallace has founded the Greater Deliverance Community Development Corporation a nonprofit community development corporation for the purpose of establishing affordable housing and economic opportunity to those that society has left behind, T.E.A.M (training effective Apostolic Ministries) and numerous other ministries for the purpose developing and strengthening ministries in Unites states and round the world.

Apostle D.L. Wallace

Greater Deliverance Global Ministries

ApostleDWallace@gmail.com

WWW. DLWallaceMinistries.com

Made in the USA
Charleston, SC
10 June 2013